D0364279

John Bailey's
BEGINNERS' Guide to
FISHING

John Bailey's
BEGINNERS' Guide to
FISHING

NH
NEW
HOLLAND

First published in 2008 by New Holland Publishers (UK) Ltd
London · Cape Town · Sydney · Auckland

Garfield House
86–88 Edgware Road
London W2 2EA
United Kingdom
www.newhollandpublishers.com

80 McKenzie Street
Cape Town 8001
South Africa

Unit 1
66 Gibbes Street
Chatswood
NSW 2067
Australia

218 Lake Road
Northcote
Auckland
New Zealand

ISBN 978 1 84773 254 5

Commissioning Editor: Ross Hilton
Design: Peter Crump
Production: Marion Storz

2 4 6 8 10 9 7 5 3 1

Reproduction by Modern Age Repro House Ltd, Hong Kong
Printed and bound by Times Offset (M) Sdn Bhd, Malaysia

CONTENTS

Understanding Fishing

If you're going to start fishing, to some degree you need a helping hand. I say, 'to some degree' because you should remember that what you experience and learn by yourself is invaluable. A perfect balance in your learning career is what you should be aiming for. I'd like this book to be your fishing friend, a constant companion, a source of inspiration, advice and confidence. If, sadly, I can't be out on the bank with you, well, this book is a substitute and, I hope, a really good one.

Father and son. Old George and young Peter. Fishing is a sport that will enchant you for many years to come.

I, OF ALL PEOPLE, KNOW HOW IMPORTANT a best fishing friend is when you're getting started. As a beginner, I had so much help myself and I still get help from my friends today. Never imagine that any angler knows it all, because it doesn't happen like that. You're always learning, or you should be. In the past, my grandmother was vital in getting me off the blocks and Ron and Pete took me on whilst still a child. As I moved into my teens Brian taught me sophistications in river techniques I'd never guessed at. Since then, I've spent years dragging information from hundreds of great anglers worldwide. Everyone you meet up with will have something to teach.

So what will you be learning from me, from this book and from others around you? Often the most important lessons revolve around the smallest of things. Slow down and don't be in too much of a hurry as you set out in the sport. Watch, take your time and work things out. Develop confidence in yourself, because that's essential. And remember that angling is a sport, something to be enjoyed and not something that should cause you heartache.

Not that it's always a sport! Sometimes it can be a matter of life and death! Let me tell you about one journey when I was grateful for all the fishing knowledge that I'd built up over the years. A mate and I were dropped off in one of the wildest parts of Greenland. As we watched the helicopter leave we knew we had the next 12 days totally on our own, totally dependent on the fish we hoped to catch. We pitched camp and, at around midday, began to fish for our supper. By 6 pm we still hadn't had a bite, or even seen one of the Arctic char that were supposed to be plentiful. We began to panic but, both being experienced travellers and anglers, we knew that wouldn't help matters. We simply thought it out. We began to realize that perhaps we'd been fishing too shallow in some of the very deep pools and, accordingly, we added a lot of weight to our flies. As we started to get down 2.5–3m (8–10ft), we began to catch fish. Soon, we had four plump char to go on the campfire. Experience saved our lives!

I'm not making the same claims of importance for this book, but what I'm hoping is that it will give you the best possible start in what is the best sport in existence. Enjoy this book and enjoy your fishing life.

There may be times on expeditions to come when cooking your catch will provide the only food for days on end. Providing your fish isn't threatened and providing you kill it humanely, members of the salmon family and sea fish especially can provide healthy, nutritious food.

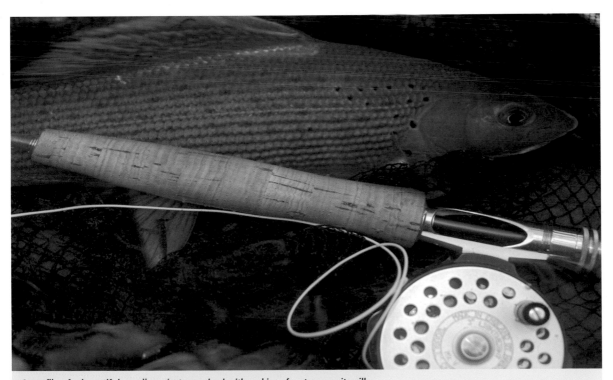

A profile of a beautiful grayling photographed with a skim of water over its gills.

Why Go Fishing?

Pauline fishes the magnificent Canadian Miramichi for Atlantic salmon. Pete is her guide, full of advice and reassurance. Remember, nobody knows it all.

For many hundreds, if not thousands, of years fishing was all about survival. After all, fish are food and a fantastic source of protein. We shouldn't forget that this is still an important factor around the world; in all continents people fish to live. In three continents I have caught fish that have helped keep people – and me – alive. And in truth, this is a basic justification for fishing. Close to the edge of life, it is an activity that can keep you and your family alive.

FOR MOST OF US, THOUGH, FISHING is a sport. Okay, there will be fish that you will decide to kill humanely and cook, you won't find a better tasting food. But a lot of the time you will be fishing for fun, for the sake of it and not for any other end.

> ❝ *To see a fish glowing in its aquatic environment is a colossal privilege.* ❞

Why fish? What's the appeal? Why bother? First, fishing introduces you to another world. Consider. Only anglers understand water, how it moves, how it works. To most people, a river is a physical feature that's as unreadable as the moon. To an angler, a river becomes an intriguing friend. And huge lakes, seas and oceans become explicable.

It's the same with fish. To those who don't fish, fish are nothing but food. They have no charm, no interest, no worth unless on a plate. To the angler, a fish is an object of enormous beauty and interest. To see a fish glowing in its aquatic environment is a colossal privilege. You gulp at the colours of fish, at their liquidity, at their grace. You begin to appreciate their lifestyle: so organized, so complete, so hidden from most of humanity in their own parallel universe.

Discovering aquatic flies As a developing angler you understand water and fish but you also learn about aquatic fly life. The whole aquatic environment becomes more comprehensible. You learn to recognize a water vole, the habits of otters, grebes, the darting kingfisher and the many different dragonflies that are drawn to the streamside where you sit.

New skills You learn exquisite skills. Fly casting is all about grace, rhythm, timing and technique. To trot a float successfully at 80–90m (260–290ft) demands huge concentration and ability. Working an artificial lure so that it looks exactly like a real prey fish is also an art.

New friends Friendship is a cornerstone of fishing. The best of fishing is all about sharing the sport. Perhaps you stalk a rising trout with a friend or you share a bag of barbel or bass. Perhaps you meet up with like-minded people on a weekend trip or an expedition to the

Jargon Buster

Trotting a float is the simple act of letting a float, with the bait underneath, move down with the current. This is a great way to cover large amounts of water and find fish. It's important to let line off the reel smoothly, so that the float moves at the same speed as the current and does not look unnatural.

wilderness. You will probably find that the best friends you ever make come through this new sport of yours. It's been that way for me.

There'll be so many personal satisfactions on your way. Of course, there'll be frustrations when you can't get a bite and disappointment when a fish breaks free, but there'll also be a sense of satisfaction when you master a new skill or outwit a difficult fish. There'll also be a sense of triumph when you land the fish of your dreams and, most of all, there'll be endless heart-stopping, white knuckle excitement as you see a fish rise to a fly, approach a bait or loom behind a lure. I've seen grown men shake, swear, sweat, sob, and dance with triumph or despair.

That's what fishing does. It strips us of all pretence and helps us rediscover the child in us all.

Good fishing is all about good friends.

Understanding Rivers

Rivers are beautiful places. Nothing quickens the heart like moving water. But a river has its secrets. It's vital to understand what the river is telling you.

Rivers are full of conflicting currents and differing depths. Take time out to form an accurate impression of what is going on.

Structure Most rivers are a series of deep pools and shallower, stony rapids. You'll often find fish feeding in the shallows before moving down to rest up in the deeper, slower, better–protected water. This is the basic structure of most rivers around the world, so learn to recognize when it's better to fish the shallower, fast water and when you should move down deeper.

Reading the river There are several major factors to take into account. You've got to consider the strength and direction of the current, the depth of the water, the amount of cover and the make-up of the riverbed. All are essential to the fish.

Current Most fish like to hang where the current isn't too strong or too slow. They need security from predators and a good food supply.

Weirs and mill pools These always attract fish. The water tumbling over the sill means that there's always oxygen. That extra depth gives security and there's always food for fish under the big stones on the bottom.

Fallen trees These are very attractive to fish. They provide shelter from attacks by water birds like cormorants. The branches harbour insects, which fall into the water and provide an added food source. And fish like the darkness and the shade from sunlight.

Rivers tend to slow and deepen on bends.

Weirs and mill pools always attract fish, partly because of shelter, depth and increased oxygen supplies.

Bridges always attract food stocks and fish are sure to follow.

Bridges They attract fish like magnets. The force of the water through the buttresses always creates a deep pool, which will be full of food. Passers-by throw rocks into the pool. Perhaps there will be a lorry wheel there. An old cart. Maybe a fridge. All these features provide shelter for the fish and attract all manner of aquatic insects, too.

Bends Always look for bends in your river. These deepest pockets of water give protection from floods in the winter and from low water levels in the summer. Food also tends to drop onto the bottom when the flow begins to decrease over the deeper part of the bend itself. The crease – that area of water between the slow eddy and the currents on the outside – always attracts fish too. Fish like to move backwards and forwards along the crease, slipping into the faster water to feed and then moving back into the slow area to rest.

Insect life falls from overhanging trees into the water and fish soon learn to look for it.

> " *Rivers are full of **character** and no two metres of river are ever the same.* "

Woods Look for areas where the river runs through a thick wood. Great. Shade from the sun in summer, protection from cold winds in the winter. And there's always lots of food falling into the water from the surrounding trees.

A big river like this is hard to read especially in the spring melt. Local guidance is important.

Man-made structures Look for old jetties, fishing platforms and other man-made structures. Fish in rivers love rocks and whilst nature provides most of these, humans often lend a hand.

Learn to regard the river like a friend. It will be sending out messages, so try to learn to read it. Rivers are full of character and no two metres of river are ever the same.

Understanding Stillwaters

At first sight, stillwaters, especially big stretches, aren't as easy to read as rivers. The features aren't quite as obvious but, with a little experience, they will begin to unfold.

Dams Lakes and reservoir dams are always a good place to start. There's deep water close in and often a lot of stonework, which boosts aquatic insect stocks. And fish always must eat!

Vegetation Never ignore weeds, reeds or lily pads. Prey fish will never be far from this type of cover and so you can always expect predators in the near vicinity. Non-predatory fish like to browse amongst vegetation where they'll find plentiful food items.

Islands These are a key feature in any stillwater. They are particularly useful to the angler when they are overhung by trees. If islands are unapproachable from the main bank, fish will love

Reeds and water weeds hold food and fish.

them for the peace and sanctuary they provide. If you can cast the necessary distance, you're in with a really big chance.

Inflows, feeder streams and springs

These are hotspots on any stillwater. It's likely that the water coming in will be well oxygenated and will probably bring in extra food as well. Springs are important. Look for where they bubble up, especially in the summer. The chances are the water will be cooler and better oxygenated and will attract fish of all species.

Bridges provide perfect observation posts.

> ❝ *Don't just settle at the first vacant swim but walk round the lake watching for signs of fish activity.* ❞

Bottom contours The bottom contours of the stillwater are vital. Deep central channels often run down the middle of lakes. They are the old streambeds from before the lake was dammed off and created. Look for plateaus, gullies and drop-offs close to the bank, especially if there are reeds and overhanging trees there.

Man-made structures Look for man-made structures. Boathouses attract perch shoals because the fish like to rub themselves on the submerged timbers. Piers and jetties are equally attractive to fish.

Observation Keep on the move. Don't just settle at the first vacant swim but walk round the lake watching for signs of fish activity. Polaroid glasses are essential. Binoculars are a help too. Look for coloured water where fish are feeding. Look for fish tails. Look for the shape of fish moving through the water. Perhaps you will see twitching reeds. Perhaps those lily pads are moving as fish glide beneath. Look for bubbles produced by feeding fish. Look at wind-chopped water. If a flat piece of water suddenly appears there, it's probably a big fish turning just beneath the surface, perhaps taking a hatching insect. Pay particular attention to the changing wind direction. Fish tend to feed on the windward shore because that's where most food is washed up.

Bulrushes attract a lot of fish species, especially tench.

John actually spotted this enormous pike before casting a surface lure to it.

Caring for Yourself

The waterside is a dangerous place; never take risks with it. Anglers drown every year around the world. Make sure that you're not one of them. Nearly all the advice I'm going to give is simple common sense. Please follow it.

Do's and don'ts Learn to swim before you go near the waterside. If you do fall in, don't panic. In a river, don't swim against the current and don't wave your arms about; keep your mouth closed and go with the flow until you can find shallows or overhanging branches to offer support. Be wary of steep banks after rain. Watch out for undercut banks, which can collapse after heavy rain. Be especially careful after dark.

Wading If you are wading in chest waders, never go too deep and be careful of fast currents. As soon as you begin to feel uneasy, stop and retrace your steps. Always wear a personal flotation device when you're wading. The best ones are lifejackets that automatically inflate within a few seconds of water immersion. A wading staff acts as a third leg and is a huge support in quick currents.

❝ *Anglers drown every year; make sure that you're not one of them.* ❞

I love to wade and to get into the water. But I always make sure the water is clear, not too deep and that the bed is firm and not silty.

Boats on freshwater These must have bailers and rowlocks, even if they have an engine too. Check weather forecasts. Take care when stepping into a boat, putting your feet on the floorboards as close to the middle as you can. Fish sitting down and don't make unexpected, abrupt movements. If a companion falls overboard don't throw him a rope without first tying a bowline (loop) in it. The loop must be big enough for the man in the water to get his head and shoulders through so that it can hold him beneath his armpits.

Boats at sea Fishing from boats at sea is even more dangerous. Join your local club for expert advice and tuition. Never go out on your own until you have complete confidence. If an engine dies, drop the anchor and stabilize the situation. Don't rely on a mobile phone for talking to lifeboats or rescue helicopters as they might have no signal out at sea. You need a properly installed VHF radio to get you through to the emergency services. You might have to wait for help, so always take lifejackets, warm clothing, food, water and flasks. Flares are essential. Familiarize yourself with your boat and its engine. Carry spares and make sure you know how to use them.

Storms and power lines Nearly all modern rods are composed of carbon fibre, which is an excellent conductor of electricity. So be careful in storms and especially careful of any overhead power lines.

Hooks Always wear Polaroids and glasses to protect your eyes and a hat to protect those vulnerable ears when you're fly-fishing. Remember that barbless hooks are not only better for the fish but, in extreme circumstances, can be much better for you as well!

Dave's always up for it, but I wouldn't advise you to take risks yourself!

Afloat in a small boat on a big water. I'm glad Ian has a top-quality lifejacket.

Caring for Fish and the Aquatic Environment

The very best anglers always care for the fish they catch. They know it's a privilege to hook, play and land something so unique, so exquisite, so beautiful. If you think carefully about every aspect of fish care you will be well on your way to becoming a better, more compassionate angler. Obey these rules and you'll tread lightly on the waters that you are fishing.

Tackle   Always make sure that your tackle is up to the challenge you are setting it. Never take chances with knots, weak line or inferior rods and reels. Make sure, too, that you stand a realistic chance of getting any fish you hook out of the piece of water you're fishing. If there seem to be too many snags, fallen trees, rocks and so on, move to a safer place. You do not ever want to leave a fish with a hook in its mouth.

Killing fish I've already talked about taking the occasional fish for the table. The act of providing fish for your family is a basic one – and an ethical one when compared with the abuses that are so common in the production of poultry and cattle. Always despatch your fish quickly and humanely with a quick, sharp blow to the back of the head, administered with a properly weighted and balanced priest. Death is painless and instant. Never take more fish than you need. Also make sure that any fish you think of killing is not rare, protected or a specimen that other people would wish to catch.

Jargon Buster

A **priest** is a manufactured tool for despatching a fish humanely. Because they are well balanced and properly designed, they are much more humane than using a rock or a branch from the river bank. If you're going to take a fish to eat, always use one.

Fish out of water Today, most fish caught on most waters are returned. Try to unhook a fish in the water without ever taking it onto the bank. You can do this with a pair of forceps, especially if your hook is semi–barbed or barbless. If a fish needs to be netted, make sure that your net is large and that the mesh is soft. Once the fish is lifted from the water, place it on something soft and damp – an unhooking mat is ideal. If you don't have one, look for moist, thick grasses. Never let a fish flap on the bank. Putting a wet cloth over its eyes is often a good way to calm it down. And always make sure that your hands are wet, especially in hot conditions.

❝ *You do not ever want to leave a fish with a hook in its mouth.* ❞

Weighing fish Only weigh fish if you must: if you think you've caught a lake record or perhaps a personal best. Always weigh a fish in a wetted, soft sling that's strong enough for the fish

Fish should be weighed quickly, efficiently and accurately. Waist slings should be soft and well wetted. Empty out all water before settling on an accurate weight. With a big fish like this, you'll need three pairs of hands.

in question. Preset the scales before putting the fish into the sling so the fish's time out of the water is reduced. Do the job with close friends and rehearse your actions with a brick so, again, time out of the water is minimized for the fish itself.

Photographs If you want to take a photograph of the fish, make sure your camera is switched on and ready to go. Support a fish as completely as possible, making sure that its stomach isn't distended or straining. Put as little pressure as possible on the fish's bone structure. Rather than the usual trophy shot, try laying a fish in the shallows or on water weeds for a more natural look. A couple of quick shots and then the fish can be straight back to the water where it belongs.

Returning fish Once the fish is ready to be returned, support it against the current in shallow water where the pace isn't too quick. Hold the fish for as long as it takes to recover. The warmer the water and the longer the fight, the more time this is going to take, so don't rush.

Wider issues Caring for fish involves more than simply looking after them once they've been hooked. As anglers, we should be watching the aquatic environment and protecting it from modern–day pressures. Remove litter. Shut gates. Obey all the rules that the riparian owners lay down. Watch out for pollution and report suspicious incidents to the relevant authorities. If your club has working parties, go along to help improve the river or stillwater. And try joining some of the conservation bodies that work tirelessly for the good of fish and fisheries all over the world.

Alberto is proud of this one hundred pound Indian mahseer. If it struggles and falls, no problem.

What Type of Fishing is for You?

With scores of different types of fishing to enjoy and fish to pursue, where exactly do you begin with this seemingly complex sport? Well, obviously, most anglers begin close to home. Whilst you're trying fishing out, seeing if you enjoy it, you might as well pursue fish that are easily within your striking range, if you'll pardon the pun! If you live in London say, there's little point in hankering after marlin off the north coast of New Zealand. These may well come your way eventually but give it time, eh?

BUT LET'S SAY YOU DO LIVE IN LONDON, or in one of the many cities around the world. There will be choices. A beginner in London, for example, can pursue coarse fish in the Thames or trout in any one of half a dozen specially stocked reservoirs. Nor is the sea far away. Everything is on the doorstep. And it's the same in many, many locations. So, to a degree, you've got to think what particularly attracts your fancy.

At this stage, what I would suggest is that you sample at least some of the wide range of opportunities open to you. Don't be in too much of a hurry to make up your mind here. This book will teach you the basics of bait, fly, lure and sea fishing, and if you're going to be really sensible, then you'll realise all types of fishing have their merit and you'll enjoy as many styles as possible. It's wrong, I believe, to be blinkered. Take carp fishing: carp are great fun but so are tench, pike, roach, bream, trout, salmon, or sea bass. It's a shame to restrict yourself to one ot two types of fish.

Just a few tips. Think hard about your holidays if you want to take up fishing. There are many places where it's possible to have a family holiday and yet do a few hours with a rod early or late in the day. Going on holiday with a fishing rod can bring you in touch with a lot of new experiences and new excitement. So keep this option in mind. Equally, think about weekends away, preferably with a tutor or a guide. You can often learn more in a day with somebody talented as an angler and a teacher than you can in a year on your own. And keep talking. Talk to as many tackle dealers as possible. Talk to people you see fishing by rivers, lakes or the seashore. The more you look and learn and experience, the more sure you will be about what you want to do with your fishing life.

Bait Fishing

In essence, bait fishing is as simple as it gets. All you've got to do is put the right bait to the right fish, in the right place at the right time, in the right way – and bingo! But, of course, any one of these five considerations can cause problems. It's always best to think every part of your approach out in every circumstance. Don't rush. Consider all the options. Above all, make a plan and stick to it until it's quite obvious that it's not working. For this reason, try always to have plans B and C cooking away in your mind as possible fallbacks if necessary.

ALWAYS GIVE YOURSELF THE EDGE. Using the very best bait is important. Remember, fish are like us. We only like nice food. We look for quality and for freshness. To a fish, a lively worm is better than a dead one. Fresh, clean maggots are better than rancid ones.

Don't underestimate your fish. Approach them carefully. Keep a low profile. Don't shout, don't run and don't wave your arms. Act like a heron; not a hooligan. Remember that once you spook a fish you just won't catch it. Chances are it won't feed again for hours.

Remember that the tackle you use will always be a factor. The fish will always be aware of it in the water around them. If the fish are pressured and the water is hard fished, they'll be really careful around your line, really watchful for your hook. If you are after wild, virgin fish, they'll be suspicious of a new, unexpected element in their environment. So, go as light with your lines and hooks as you can. Make sure, though, you're not going so light that you risk losing the fish you're after. You don't want too heavy a float or weight but they mustn't be so light that they won't hold their position in the current or you can't cast to where the fish are. Tackle choice, therefore, is all a question of compromise.

Stealth is everything. Don't spook the fish.

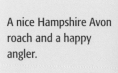

A nice Hampshire Avon roach and a happy angler.

Tackle Shop

It's desperately important that you don't waste money, at this early stage, on the wrong fishing tackle. Get your tackle right and fishing will be a pleasure; get it wrong and fishing can be a misery. So how do you start?

Gather information Read reviews on tackle in magazines and fishing papers. Talk to anglers on the bank. Look at what they are using and ask them how they like it. If you can, try rods out in an actual fishing situation. It's good to know how they perform on the riverbank and not just in a shop. When you do go to a fishing tackle shop, don't be afraid to ask questions. The staff are there to help; if they don't, go somewhere else. It helps them if you have a clear idea of the waters you will be fishing and the species you'll be after. Don't always buy on the Internet. Prices might look attractive but you could pick up an item of tackle

that really isn't what you want and an exchange could be problematic. If you build up a good relationship with your tackle dealer it can last for life and bring you nothing but benefits.

Rods There is a startling choice of fishing rods available on the market today. Take a deep breath and think carefully. For a start, go for the best rod you can afford. You do get what you pay for and if you can afford a decent rod straight off, it will be a friend for life. Always look for a lifetime guarantee on a rod. If you break a piece of it, there might be a service charge but at least the rod is not totally defunct. At this early stage in your career, whatever purpose you have for a rod in your mind, choose a good all-rounder. For example, if you're carp fishing, go for a 3.6m (12ft), 1kg (2½lb) test curve model. This, you will find, is a good

Lee blinds up an accurate long range cast.

casting rod that also works well close in. If you're looking for a float rod, go for a nice actioned 4m (13ft) model. You will find that this is not too long and not too short; and will be perfect for all types of fishing. Consider an Avon style 3.4m (11ft) legering rod. You can use this on rivers for barbel and chub and on stillwaters for tench and carp. At a push, it can even become a light spinning rod. Specialized rods are good for specific purposes but you can build up an armoury of these rods as you progress. If you want to choose just a single bait-fishing rod then I would go for that 3.4m (11ft) Avon. I use mine for 80 per cent of my bait fishing and some sea fishing as well.

Reels   A fixed spool reel is the norm these days. It's tempting to choose one that is too big. Make sure your reel balances the rod nicely. Don't think you have to have a 'bait runner' facility –

these are only really useful in carp fishing. Once again, buy the best reel you can afford. This will give you a smooth clutch for playing a fish, durability and a smooth rewind. Centre pin reels are more specialized and great for river work. They are beautiful to use and to fish with but a fixed spool reel will trot a float satisfactorily at the early stages of your career. Only consider a centre pin if most of your fishing will be on rivers.

Centre pin reels are very traditional but also very effective.

Lines There are specialized types of nylon line, such as copolymers and fluorocarbons but, at this early stage, I would go for a steady, traditional, monofilament. Maxima is the world standard. Buy a variety of breaking strains so that you can cope with light, medium and heavier work. The bulk of my fishing is done with 1.4kg (3lb), 2.3kg (5lb), 3.6kg (8lb) and 5kg (12lb) breaking strain. Occasionally you need to go heavier than that but rarely when you're starting out. There are also many types of braid line on the market. Braid does have advantages: it's very strong for its diameter and it's very limp. However, it also has its own set of problems and I'd avoid it early in your career.

Hooks As a general rule, buy barbless hooks. If you do buy barbed, you can always press the barb down with a pair of forceps. Barbless hooks are always easier to get out of a fish and, from time to time, yourself! You'll need a range of sizes to give you options. Remember you always need to relate your hook size to your bait. For example, a size 20 hook with a single maggot, a size 16 with two maggots, a size 12 with one grain of corn, a size 10 with a medium worm, a size 8 with a piece of bread flake, a size 6 with a boilie, a pellet or a piece of luncheon meat. Keep your hooks dry. If you store them where they can get wet, they will soon go rusty and be useless.

Floats There's a difference between river and stillwater floats. Stillwater floats tend to be thin-bodied wagglers that are very delicate and sensitive. River floats often have cork bodies, which are bulbous and give the float more buoyancy to help it ride the current, although you can fish wagglers in slower-moving rivers. Once again, go for a range of floats so you can fish light and heavy, close in and further out, in slow currents and quicker ones, in windy conditions and still. Although red is nearly always good for visibility, it pays to buy a range of colours. You'll need float rubbers to attach your float to the line and split shot to cock the float. Split shot is not made of toxic lead anymore out of respect for waterfowl and the environment.

weight?

Legers and swim feeders If you're fishing with a bait hard on the bottom, you will need a range of leger weights and swim feeders. We will be discussing this style of fishing later (see pages 38–41) but just remember, once again, to get a range of both. Weights generally range from a 4g (⅛oz) up, in extreme circumstances, to 60g (2oz).

❝ Get your tackle right and fishing will be a pleasure; get it wrong and fishing can be a misery. ❞

Float fishing in amongst the reeds is an excellent way at getting to roach and big perch.

A superb tench caught courtesy of a small block end feeder.

Rod rests, bobbins and bite alarms

Rod rests are useful, along with bobbins and bite alarms, but these are at the sophisticated end of the market and you probably don't need them when you are starting out.

Everything else

You'll need luggage to carry everything in. Buy something rugged and hardwearing. The last thing you want is breaking straps or tearing canvas. You will probably need a catapult to fire your bait out. You will need a landing net for that magical moment when your first decent fish comes to the bank. Buy quality and don't go too small. You will need forceps so you can flick the hook out of the fish's mouth. An unhooking mat is also a great idea. You wet the mat and place your fish on it so it can't come to harm. There are a host of other, smaller items, which you will find you build up in the months and seasons to come. For example, I'd never fish anywhere without my Leatherman multi-tool; this amazing piece of kit has proved its worth on thousands of occasions.

Halibut pellets are one of the big baits of the new century. Attach them to the hook with glued elastic bands.

Clothing

No matter what type of fishing you do, the clothing you wear is absolutely essential. If you don't wear the proper clothing, you simply won't enjoy your fishing. The very best clothing ranges today are modular, designed around the layer system, and created in the most hi-tech of modern fabrics.

Base layer This is made from fast-drying, hardwearing synthetic fibres and worn next to the skin. It keeps you comfortable by wicking moisture away from your body. Let's say you're walking the riverbank, using lures for bass or pike. You use energy and begin to sweat. If this moisture stays near the skin, you will start to feel cold, especially when you stop walking. The wicking fabrics in the base layer move this moisture to the next layer of the system. The best base-layer garments are insulating, close-fitting, soft and warm.

Middle layer These garments are made from fabrics that trap and hold the warm air created by your body. They also move moisture to the outer layer of your clothing. The primary choice for mid-layer fabric is polyester fleece as this is lightweight, durable, has very low water absorbency, dries quickly and moves moisture fast. Windproof fleece fabric has the added advantage of preventing wind chill and giving protection from light rain.

Final layer This layer, often referred to as a shell, provides protection against the elements, especially wind and rain, and helps to release moisture from the previous layer. The shell needs to keep out the rain and wind whilst retaining heat in the two layers beneath.

Obviously, the more money you spend, the better the quality and durability of the clothing. Look also for useful features, such as strong zips good hoods, hand pockets with warm-feel liners, internal pockets and waist adjustments. If you plan to fly-fish, you may want to consider buying a vest. This is clothing for life, so take your time and choose the best.

Chest waders

I'm a great believer in breathable chest waders, even if you're not going to wade in your local waters. It doesn't matter how wet the day becomes, if you've got a good outer shell jacket and chest waders beneath, there is no way wind, snow or sleet is ever going to penetrate. If it's cold, you simply put on an extra pair of base-layer trousers. If it's hot, you can still walk for miles in good, breathable chest waders, they'll feel just like a normal pair of pants. Also, having a completely waterproof bottom, you can sit on a wet bankside in total comfort.

Neoprene chest waders are cheaper and they are fine in very cold conditions if you're not doing much walking. However, the problem with neoprene is that you can't ever get cool in it, so if you're going to be active or if you want to wear them during the warmer months, you may come to regret your choice.

" If you don't wear the proper clothing, you simply won't enjoy your fishing. "

Boots

Team up your chest waders with really good boots and you can wade safely and walk miles in comfort. Be careful with the soles of the boots. Probably my favourite is a felt sole with plenty of stainless steel studs embedded. Rubber cleating is also good.

Head covering

In cold conditions, most of your heat escapes your body through your head, so make sure you have real insulation up there where it counts. I always like to wear a thermal-type hat underneath the hood of my shell garment. This way my head remains warm as well as dry.

Polaroid glasses

And don't forget your Polaroid glasses. They are essential if you are going to see beneath the surface layer into the water. They are particularly essential if you're fly-fishing. Nobody wants to have unprotected eyes if a fly is hurtling close to the head at high speed!

Breathable chest waders let you get out into the water closer to your fish.

Perfectly kitted out. Light. Breathable. Waterproof. Windproof.

Understanding Bait-Caught Fish

You might think that using bait puts you ahead of the game compared with artificial flies or lures. This is not necessarily so. To get the very best out of your sessions you've really got to get into the head of bait-caught fish.

Natural baits These often work far better than anything you can buy or make. Remember that the vast majority of fish eat natural foodstuffs most of the time in most waters. Caddis grubs, in particular, can make great baits. Try two or three of them on a size 14 or 16 hook. Worms are great after rain. You wouldn't believe how many get washed into your average river, where the fish can gorge on them. Try slugs off your lettuce patch. Use your imagination but don't use any living creature that is rare, endangered or protected.

Bait size Sometimes there is so much natural food in a water that the fish become preoccupied with it to the exclusion of everything else. In the late summer, for example, huge shoals of daphnia drift in the water. These microscopic organisms are hoovered up by fish of every species. At times like this a big bait can very occasionally work, simply by providing a shock–tactic approach. A better, safer bet is to use small baits in big numbers. Maggots, hemp seed and casters (the chysalis stage

between maggots and bluebottles) are great for this style of work.

Smelly baits In coloured water fish have a great problem in actually seeing your baits. This is where big, smelly baits come in. Luncheon meat is the perfect example. And don't be shy about using a big, big piece. Sometimes you can use even a quarter of the can as a single bait. Or try using three or four really big pieces up the line from the hook. Make an impact.

Modern or traditional? Modern baits like boilies, pellets and special pastes (see pages 30–33) are all very good. The trouble is, sometimes they are used to the exclusion of everything else on the water and the fish learn very quickly. If you suspect the fish are wising up, try something different. You can often go back to an old favourite like sweetcorn with great success.

> ❝ To get the very best out of your sessions you've really got to get into the head of bait-caught fish. ❞

A stunning tench is held a second before release.

Be different It always pays to try something different. Put two or three pellets on the hook and not just one. Use a huge piece of paste instead of a normal–sized one. Or a tiny piece of paste perhaps. If you're different and stand out from the crowd, you might just fool a fish when everything else fails.

How much bait? Don't overfeed. It's easy to throw bait in but it's not as easy to take it out. Suss out how the fish are reacting to the feed. Did fish initially come on but did your bites then tail off? Perhaps they are not hungry and you're just putting too much out there. Remember, too, that a single succulent bait is often enough to attract a response; you don't always need loose feed round it. Be especially careful of overfeeding in cold, clear, bright conditions.

Loose feed Be very careful about introducing loose feed – especially heavy items like boilies and pellets – over fish feeding in shallow water. Sound travels very quickly underwater and a cascade of pellets going in really makes a commotion.

Timing Most fish feed at dawn and dusk but this isn't always the case. If you can get to the water at dawn, in particular, you might well see feeding fish. But always read the signs. Look for bubbles bursting on the surface, for stained water, for tailing fish, for twitching reeds as fish put in and lily pads trembling as fish forage beneath them.

Choosing your swim Above all, always read the water and take your time before settling into a swim. And remember, fish don't like feeding over dirty riverbeds so look for clean gravel, sand or stones.

Common Freshwater Bait-Caught Fish	
UK & Europe	Barbel
Common Carp	Pike
Mirror Carp	Perch
Crucian Carp	
Tench	**North America**
Bream	Catfish
Roach	Yellow Perch
Rudd	Pan Fish
Eels	Walleye
Dace	Bullhead
Chub	Striped Bass

A very pretty dace comes to the bank.

The author is justifiably proud of a fine, river-caught common carp.

Skills of Baiting

Get your bait as right as you possibly can and you're halfway to catching that fish. Let's take something as humble as luncheon meat. Most people use pieces the size of a thumbnail. But fish soon realize that spells danger. Instead, use a tiny piece of meat, just enough to cover the small hook. Or let's say the water is really cloudy. Use a huge piece, perhaps even a quarter to a third of a tin. Try, also, pulling the meat to bits with your fingers so there are lots of loose edges. This way tiny bits disappear off into the water and spread the smell. Most people cut meat with a knife so it's uniform: the fish get to recognize the neat shape as well.

Pre-baiting By pre-baiting I mean putting free offerings of bait into the swim to get the fish used to it before you actually begin to fish. You can pre-bait for weeks. Sometime pre-baiting the day before you fish can work. On other occasions you can put bait into the swim at 9am and return at 10 or 11pm and find the fish totally switched on to it. One of the skills is pre-baiting exactly the right amount. You don't want to fill the fish up before you arrive but equally you've got to bait up enough to get them eagerly looking for what you are offering.

Carp adore floating baits. This is a fish approaching confidently from beneath.

Bread So let's look at types of bait in detail. Baits from the kitchen have proved some of the most popular for centuries. You can't beat bread. It can be used in crust, flake or paste forms. Fish all over the world recognize and like the taste of bread. And, being white, it is easily seen both in flooding water and at night. The great thing about bread is that it is so adaptable. You can use big or small pieces. You can use floating crust on the surface or tether bits of crust to the bottom. If the fish are wary of flake, you can wet the bread and mould it into a paste. And you can flavour the paste, too. Perhaps add some cheese or custard powder.

Cheese This bait has always been a winner. You can use it on its own or made into a bread paste. Soft cheese, hard cheese, cream cheese and processed cheese all work incredibly well.

It often helps to fool a carp if your floating bait is positioned in thick weed beds so the line is hidden from the approaching fish.

❝ Get your bait as right as you possibly can and you're halfway to catching that fish. ❞

Bait Selection

1 Bread
Use your loaf... sliced bread is a perfect hookbait.

2 Sausage
Cooked sausage can be cut into slices.

3 Luncheon meat
This can be cut into any shape and stays on the hook well.

4 Cheese spread
Creates an excellent bait when mixed into a paste with bread.

5 Crusts
Chunks of floating crust are especially good for carp.

6 Sweetcorn
This is an effective bait for most non-predatory fish species.

7 Fruit
Even the humble banana will attract fish such as chub.

Particle baits Some 30 years ago, the angling world found sweetcorn and what a great bait that has proved in the decades since for all manner of cyprinids (a large family of fish, including carp). Use the grains singly or in bunches. Or try the modern flavoured corn. Red corn can work well, as can black.

Turn over any rock or stone in a fertile river and you will find clusters of natural bait underneath.

One of the great appeals of sweetcorn is that it is what we call a particle bait. Particle baits are small baits that you use in great numbers. Baits such as maggots, hemp seed, nuts, sweetcorn, casters and tares (one of the many forms of seed bait) all preoccupy the fish and, at times, drive them into a feeding frenzy. The fish often become so focused on tiny baits that they won't look at larger ones. At this stage in your career, you will probably find that maggots, casters, hemp seed and sweetcorn are pretty much all you need.

Worms Of course, most fish eat natural baits most of the time – especially in non–commercial waters. It makes sense to give the fish exactly what they're looking for in their own world. Worms can't be beaten. You can buy worms commercially or pick them from the surface of any grassland on a warm, moist night. It pays to look after your worms, keeping them damp and throwing away any dead or dying ones. Worms are especially good after heavy rains when lakes and stillwaters are coloured and lots of worms have been washed off surrounding pasture. You can chop worms up into many small pieces and mix them with fine soil. The resulting smelly cloud will send most fish species crazy. Slugs, leeches, crickets, caddis grubs, grasshoppers, moths... any natural creature is going to entice a fish which is looking constantly for what nature can bring it.

Specialized baits In this modern, commercially driven age there are also many specialized baits. Over the past 20 years or so these have tended to dominate the market. Boiled baits, or boilies, are the best known. They are used on the hook or as a free offering. Boilies are carefully prepared and chemically based. They have great smells, great colourings and are very nutritious. As a result, boilies dominate the carp–fishing market. Boilies are usually made by adding dried powder to eggs and flavouring. The mixture is made into a paste, rolled into balls and boiled to give a hard skin. Boilies are based on high–protein mixes with all manner of essences and additions to make them taste, smell and look great. You can make boilies buoyant so they pop up off the bottom. Mini–boilies act very much like particles. So you see there are a wide range to use.

Almost as popular today as boilies are fishmeal–based pellets. These are generally hard and fished either on a hair or with a plastic band around them. They are particularly good for carp and all manner of river fish.

The contents of a carp fisher's bucket can be intriguing. The boilies are cut in half to release more smell. One ingredient, hemp seed, is oily and terrifically aromatic.

Ground bait There will be times when you need to use what we call ground bait. The oldest, most commonly used form of ground bait is simply breadcrumbs, which you wet and make into balls. These balls can be laced with hemp seed, maggots or casters and catapulted into the swim. As they hit the water they explode into a tantalizing cloud. Today, new ground baits have all kinds of different additives, which increase scent and visual attractiveness. Go into any tackle shop and you will find the choice bewildering.

When you are mixing ground bait, make sure to get the consistency correct. Light ground bait can be used for shallow stillwaters, whereas heavier ground bait will be needed for quick, deep rivers. Mix your ground bait up, drop it into the water and see how it behaves. If it sinks stone–like to the bottom, you've got to fluff it up and use less water.

When you are putting ground bait in, it pays to use more smaller balls rather than a few very heavy ones. There's always a risk of scaring the fish if you bombard the area in front of you – especially if it's shallow and the fish are skittish. Really, ground baiting is like everything else in this new, exciting sport. It demands that you think carefully and don't do anything that might scare the fish.

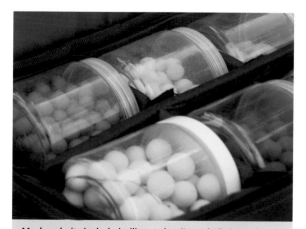

Modern baits include boilies and pellets of all sizes, shapes, colours and flavours.

Float Fishing

The basic rule is always to choose a float that is heavy enough for the job in hand. Providing you shot the float properly, even a small fish will have no problem pulling it under. A big float is easier to cast and easier to control. If you go too light, both these important functions become difficult.

REMEMBER, TOO, that floats come in all sorts of different shapes. Broadly speaking, bodied floats – those that aren't straight – are more buoyant and are designed for river work. Straight floats – like wagglers – are more suited to stillwaters or very slow-moving rivers.

A float is primarily used to signal a bite from a fish, so it has to be visible. Most of my floats have red tips because they really do stand out. But remember, too, that floats also are useful for suspending baits at different levels in the water. You don't always want a bait on the bottom and if you want to fish in mid-water or above, you simply have to use a float to suspend it. Floats are beautiful things and you'll enjoy watching them. They're even more beautiful when they disappear under the surface.

Floats in Running Water

Which float? Common river floats are Avons, which have a good thick body and are perfect for trotting quick water at longish distances. Most river fishing, though, is done with stick floats, which are attached to the line at the top and the bottom. They give perfect control in slower water over shorter distances. With Avons and sticks, you've really got enough choice of floats to cover virtually all water conditions.

Shotting Attaching shot to the float is very important. You need to put enough shot on the line so that the float cocks and only the tip shows above the surface. When you're stick–float fishing, the shot is spread pretty evenly from the float down to the hook. When you are using an Avon float, you can group the shot midway between float and hook. This lets the float ride well in the current.

Long trotting This is one of the nicest ways to use a float on the river. It's an ideal way of exploring long stretches because you can let the float amble down with the current a good 80m (260ft) or more. This allows you to get near to spooky fish on very clear water. You need a long rod for this type of fishing – a modern, light, 4.5m (15ft) rod is ideal. Mostly, you will be using lines between 1.4kg and 2.7 kg (3lb and 6lb) breaking strain for fish like roach, chub, grayling and even barbel. When you are long trotting, it's important to 'mend' the line. That's simply keeping direct contact from the rod to the float and not allowing great loops of line to develop on the current. If you don't mend the line, the float will get pushed off course and the bait will behave unnaturally.

Getting in the river (safely) with the flow behind you allows you to control a float much more easily.

Long-trotting technique Control the float thoughtfully and guide it towards snags and fish-holding features. Hold the float back – that simply means stopping the line so that the float can't travel and the bait tends to lift up in the water. This is often a critical moment, so expect a bite. If you're fishing at long range, you'll really have to put some beef into the strike because you've got to pick up a lot of line and set the hook.

It doesn't always pay to go for the most comfortable place to fish. Think carefully about where the best attack points are going to be. Work out a strategy in your head and consider how you're going to land any fish hooked.

Notice how this float is just being held back a little bit. This allows the bait to rise enticingly in the water, in front of the fish's nose.

Stick-float fishing This is more intimate and is better for slower swims, which are often quite deep. When you're stick–float fishing, baiting is vital. It often pays to feed small amounts of maggots, casters or hemp at virtually every cast. Make sure you put in this loose feed well upstream so it settles in the area of the river you're actually fishing.

Stick-float fishing technique Like long trotting, when you're stick–float fishing, it's important to keep the line direct from the rod tip to the float and to maintain constant control. Hold the float back, so that the bait rises up from the bottom – an action fish can't resist.

" *Floats are beautiful things and you'll enjoy watching them. They're even more beautiful when they disappear under the surface.* "

Stillwater Float Fishing

Wagglers Wagglers are the most commonly used freshwater floats. They are long and slim and sometimes transparent, so that fish don't see them as easily in shallow, clear water. Wagglers are attached to the line by the bottom end only. These floats are ideal for all stillwater work. You can fish your bait as it falls through the water simply by pushing the shot up towards the float.

Shot Stillwaters are never actually still and are always being pushed around by winds and currents. If you're having trouble keeping your float in one position, it often pays to put a small shot 15–30cm (6–12in) up the line from the float. This sinks the line underneath the surface and makes the float easier to control.

Casting Let's say you've baited up a swim 10m (30ft) out with loose feed, maggots, sweetcorn and the like and/or ground bait. It's a good idea to cast the float 15m or even 20m (50–65ft) from the bank and then reel it in to the baited area. This is because it sometimes disturbs feeding fish if you cast the float directly in over their heads.

The bite You will find that different species of fish bite in different ways. For example, tench bites often take a long time to really develop. The float will often twitch, tremor, rise up in the water, sometimes fall flat and then finally shoot away under.

Finding feeding fish When you're fishing a waggler in a stillwater, look for signs of feeding fish. Bubbles rising to the surface are the most common. Tench produce small, pin–sized bubbles. With carp and bream, the bubbles are larger and more spasmodic. Look, too, for coloured water – a sure sign that fish are down there feeding.

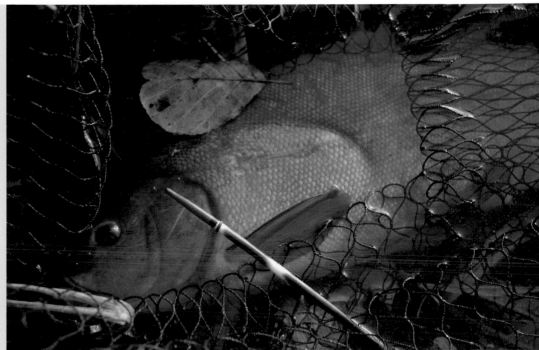

A fine tench caught on a traditional quill float. These are alternatives to the modern plastic waggler.

This great perch was caught on float-fished worm. The buoyant float used was perfect for big bait in fast water.

Legering

Sometimes it's important that your bait is moving and, on the river, that's why you'll frequently use a float. However, on both stillwater and rivers, it can be vital to put the bait hard on the bottom where the fish are often feeding. A bait suspended in mid-water simply won't be looked at. To do this, you either use a straight leger weight, or lead, or employ the use of a swim feeder.

OF COURSE, WITHOUT A FLOAT, you've got to see the bite develop. There are several ways of registering this. Sometimes you will use a very sensitive rod tip – generally a quiver tip – which shows up exactly what is happening on your bait. Sometimes you will use a butt indicator. You clip this on the line between your reel and the bottom ring. When the fish bites, the butt indicator moves towards the rod. Sounds easy, doesn't it? Well, there are a few complications.

Swim Feeders

A swim feeder has an added advantage in that you can pack it with ground bait and loose samples of hook bait to attract the fish.

Casting When you're using a feeder, make sure your casting is tight and always on the same spot. What you don't want to do is spread your ground bait loosely around a large area. This breaks the fish up when you are looking to concentrate them. The easiest way to make sure your casting is this accurate is to choose a feature on the opposite bank, whether you're fishing a lake or a river, and cast to it, always keeping on the same line. As for distance, you can put a bit of tape on your spool once you've cast out so you'll be reaching exactly the same spot cast after cast. I can't emphasize accuracy enough.

> ## Jargon Busting
>
> **Legering** is the simple act of fishing a bait hard on the bottom for fish that are expected to feed there. A simple lead or a swim feeder are generally the weights used to keep the bait anchored.

Entering the water When your feeder enters the water, you don't want it to go in with a big splash, especially in shallow, clear water. You can 'feather' it down as it approaches the water. Feathering really means dabbing your finger on the reel spool as the line comes off it. This tends to slow the feeder down in flight and make its entry less splashy.

Bites Hitting those bites can be difficult. Mostly you will be watching the quiver tip, as that's the normal tool to use when feeder fishing. Sometimes a tip will pull right round, but frequently it won't. Often all you will see is flickers and nudges. Keep experimenting until you start hitting those bites. Try hitting just nudges and trembles. If that doesn't work, sit on your hands and wait for a bite to develop. Alternatively, vary the hook length you are using – that's the distance

This really nice chub was caught on the bottom on a light leger moving slowly with the current.

between the hook and the feeder. Sometimes it pays to go from 30cm (1ft) to 60cm (2ft) or even 1.2m (4ft). Change your hook size. If you are using two maggots, try one or three. Try adding a small red worm to the bait. Keep at it and you will find the solution.

Lead Weights

Swim feeders aren't always the answer because they are bulky and can disturb the fish. Sometimes it's easier and more practical to use a simple lead weight. This applies to both rivers and stillwaters.

Size On rivers especially, the size of the lead is critical. You want it just to hold bottom and not get swept away by the current. However, at the same time, you don't want to use too heavy a lead on either rivers or stillwaters because of the splash.

Bait If you're not using a swim feeder but a straight lead, then you've got to attract the fish to your bait. This can be done by using free samples of the hook bait thrown into the stillwater or river, or by using ground bait. Mostly, nowadays, you'll be buying a ground bait mix from a tackle shop. Read the instructions carefully because you've got to get the mix absolutely right. You don't want to

make it too wet so that the balls break up in the air and scatter all over the water. Equally, you don't want to mix it too dry so it goes in like a stone. The ideal is for the balls to break up as they hit the surface. They will then dissolve all the way to the bottom, creating a curtain of attraction.

Big Bait

There are times when you can get away with substituting a lead or a swim feeder with big baits. What I'm thinking of here is perhaps one or two lobworms on the hook, or a piece of luncheon meat, or cheese, or bread flake. If the bait you've got has real weight to it, you can cast it a long way and it will hold bottom even in flowing water. A bait fished like this is particularly attractive to big, wary fish. Everything seems much more natural.

Bites Detecting bites when using a big, single bait is often quite easy. Sometimes the line will simply tighten and you will watch it move across the water's surface. Often a big fish takes a big bait with gusto so the rod tip will move round. You can also touch leger. To touch leger, you hold the rod in one hand and the line, close to the reel, in the fingers of the other. You then feel – or touch – for a bite. Sometimes this bite can be a simple tug,

It's a good idea to build up a whole collection of different sized weights in different designs. This is a specialist angler's collection, housed in a specifically designed bag. Don't use too heavy a weight. In rivers, it should just keep its position in the current.

The feeder obviously gets samples of bait to the bottom in close vicinity to the hook. It can, therefore, be a useful tool but be careful in shallow, clear water where the splash of entry is a problem and where it's very obvious. The feeder, too, is more likely to work with naïve than pressured fish.

" *It can be vital to put the bait hard on the bottom where the fish are often feeding.* "

sometimes a strong pull, and sometimes a build up of pressure. If this sounds complicated, don't worry! Experience will quickly make you a master. This is a really convenient way of fishing and very sensitive and exciting. If you point your rod tip directly to where you think your bait is lying, this type of indication will be all the more powerful.

Good touch legering technique is all about comfort.

This barbel is being held in the current until its strength is fully returned to swim away safely. Otherwise it would simply be swept away, turned belly up and, in all probability, drown. Remember, too, that the less time any fish spends out of the water the shorter the recuperation time needed.

Problem Busting

66 *The carp in my local water seem to be very wary of the floating baits that I like to use. Any ideas?* 99

Carp soon wise up to surface–fished baits. Going lighter in line, or perhaps using fluorocarbon, which is very strong for its diameter, can sometimes help. Fluorocarbon is also good because it sinks beneath the surface and is partly disguised. However, don't go too light or you will be in trouble. Often, carp learn to suss out the bait with a hook attached to it because there are lots of free offerings to compare it with. Sometimes, therefore, it's a good idea just to cast out a single bait on a hook. Too many baits also make carp fussy and overfed. If there's just one bait, they are likely to be hungry and competitive. Also, try one large, single bait like a piece of floating crust. Carp will see it and, being large, it will hide the hook very well.

Think about where you fish your floater. Out into a strong ripple is good as the distorted water surface breaks up the profile of the line. Or fish close in to reeds and lily beds. Sometimes, reeds tied onto the last 30cm (12in) or so of line can disguise its shape. Best of all, get the fish feeding right in the margins and you can dangle a piece of floater vertically under your rod tip with no line on the surface at all. And how exciting is that!

66 *The tench seem to eat all my free offerings but then go and leave my hook bait… help.* 99

What's happening is that the tench are browsing just off the bottom, sucking in bait. The loose feed goes into their mouths but bait with a hook in proves too heavy and stays where it is on the bed. What you need to do is make the bait that you're using float up into the tench's mouth as it sucks. A hair rig will do this. So will floating casters. Check

A carp comes confidently to a bait without a hook. The problem comes when it sees the line.

Jargon Buster

A **hair rig** is the act of putting a bait on a hair tied to the hook, rather than putting the bait on the hook itself. Without the weight of the hook tethering it, a bait can rise easily and naturally into the mouth of a fish sucking at it from above.

Rob has a really good carp on the end here but it's moving to his right, heading for thick reed beds. He's putting pressure on and changing the angle of his pull. Have faith in the strength of your tackle and remember it's best to push it to its limits than let a fish find a snag and freedom.

them out in a bowl of water. Use a couple that are floating on a size 12 hook and you will find that they counterbalance the weight of the metal. You can also buy plastic, imitation particle baits. So, for example, use a size 14 hook with a piece of real sweetcorn and add a piece of plastic sweetcorn. This will increase the buoyancy and allow the tench to suck the hook in. Alternatively, go for a big, heavy bait that the tench literally have to pick up. A big lobworm, perhaps, or a large pellet.

Crucian carp are one of the most delightful of our bait-caught species. Though not big, they're beautiful and very cunning.

> **❝** *I've got a great Crucian Carp water near me but they're driving me mad. I can't seem to get anything more than dithery bites.* **❞**

Crucians are weird fish. What they like to do is suck and blow at a bait until it's soft enough to take between the lips and swallow. This means that you get these long periods when the float simply quivers and dips without doing anything decisive. My advice is to use soft baits if at all possible. Perhaps a piece of soft paste, or maggots that are already half sucked out. Alternatively, go for very small baits. Perhaps half a grain of sweetcorn. Crucians love ground bait that's hemp based. Mix up a little bit very stiffly and try that on the hook. Or try just a tip of redworm – 6mm (¼in) is quite enough. Make sure your hook isn't too big. Crucians rarely grow above 1.3kg (3lb) in weight so a size 16 is probably as large as you need go.

❝ *Should I use less feed in the winter?* ❞

Difficult one. If the water is very clear and cold and there is a period of high pressure, it's very possible that most of the cyprinid species will slow down their metabolism and feed less. So that means that you use less ground bait and less loose feed if you want to avoid filling them up. Alternatively, if there's a period of warm, low pressure with lots of wind and rain, you'll find cyprinids like carp and bream come on the feed very strongly. If they haven't fed for two or three weeks, they might be ravenous and quite a lot of food is going to be necessary to attract and hold them. But it's a great question; it shows that you are thinking about how the fish live and behave – and that's the core of what fishing is all about.

Use all the natural cover that you can to get close to your fish.

River species love marginal weed growth and overhanging trees. Always remember that food and shelter are top issues in any fish's thinking.

66 *I'm missing too many bites. What should I do?* 99

Well, probably the first thing to try out is using smaller hooks and smaller hook baits. It could be that the fish are just too small to get a big bait into their mouths. Or, it could be that the fish are wary and a big bait and a big hook is making them bite in a tentative fashion. Failing that, you can try leaving the bite a bit longer and waiting to see if it's going to develop. Sometimes fish like bream and tench like to mouth a bait for a good few seconds before deciding whether to swallow it. If this is the case, striking too early simply pulls a bait out from their lips. The one fish that you don't want to try this method with is the perch. If you leave a bait too long when the perch are biting, they'll simply gorge it and you will have a dead fish on your hands.

66 *When I'm float fishing on stillwaters and it's breezy, I find a lot of surface drift pulls the float from where I want to hold it.* 99

Stillwater is a total misnomer. All stillwaters have currents and countercurrents working in them, even small ones. Sometimes, it can be an advantage to have your float moving slowly across the surface of the water, pushed by the breeze. It means that deep down your hook and bait is exploring more of the underwater terrain and possibly locating more fish. Mostly, though, it's something to be avoided. You could try a backstop. This is simply a small shot placed up the line above the float. Mostly, a tiny shot will do the job and sink the line between the float and the rod tip. This makes it much less vulnerable to surface drift. Or you can soak your line in a mixture made from washing-up liquid and a few drops of water. The washing-up liquid makes line sink like a stone. It

also helps if you plunge your rod tip under the surface of the water as soon as the float has landed and tighten up to it. You will find that the line stays under the water and avoid drift this way.

66 *My lakes are very clear indeed and though I can see the fish, I just can't get bites.* 99

If your fish are big and they know all about anglers' wiles, it can be very difficult to catch them when the water is very clear, especially in bright sunlight. If you try fishing for them early in the morning, at dusk or into night, you will find there is less light for them to see by. This in itself is a great bonus. Windy days are a big help. If the lakes are large, wind can stir up the bottom, colouring the water, which makes your terminal tackle less easy for the fish to detect. Equally, if there's heavy rain, the crystal-clear nature of the water will become clouded and fish will feed with much less caution. Failing all this, you will just have to use lighter line and smaller hooks, probably with a minimum of loose feed. Look, too, for areas where fish feel safer. These can be close to snags, under overhanging trees or close to dense weed beds. If fish are in open, clear water, their guard is high.

If you see carp moving slowly along the bottom then they're probably feeding. When they dig for food they tip up so that the tail rises in the water.

" I can't cast as far as other people seem to be doing. "

It could be that your rod is too short or doesn't have the power to cast a long way. Perhaps your line is too thick. Heavy line is less easy to cast than lighter line – though you should never go so light as to run the risk of losing tackle or a hooked fish. Perhaps you're not using enough weight. Perhaps a heavier float, lead or swim feeder would do the job. Perhaps your technique needs refining a bit. Remember that timing is all important if you are trying to cast long distances. But also, consider whether long casting is actually necessary at all. Just because everybody else is casting long distances doesn't mean to say that you've got to. It could be that if you fished the margins – which everyone else is ignoring – you could be in for some surprises. Don't always follow the herd.

Lee is an expert caster. Everything is done in a quiet, confident, controlled fashion. Here he lines up his cast, preparing for the lift off.

" Every time I hook a big fish I seem to lose it. "

First of all, you've got to consider your tackle. Is the line heavy enough? Is the rod up to the job in hand? Is the clutch on your reel set correctly? It should give under moderate pressure. Are your knots totally secure? Is your hook big enough and strong enough? Next, you've got to consider where you are fishing. Are you too close to reeds, fallen trees, boulders or other snags? Are you actually giving yourself a feasible chance of extracting a good fish from a difficult, snag–ridden area? Thirdly, you've got to consider your technique. Make sure you keep the rod high when you're playing a fish. Don't let the point drift down towards the water. Remember the rod has lots of give in it so that it can bend to the pressure of a running fish. When a fish runs, let it go – providing it's not too close to snags. If you clamp down hard on a big fish moving fast, a break is inevitable. Take especial care when a fish is coming close to the net. When it sees you, there's bound to be another run for sanctuary. If the clutch of your reel is set too tight, this could be a moment of disaster. And, finally, make sure your net is big enough for the fish you are pursuing. Don't pursue a tired fish with the net – this will only alarm it. Keep the net in position and draw the beaten fish over it. Once you are sure everything is in position, lift and the fish is yours.

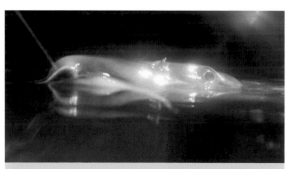

When you're landing barbel, always be prepared for a last rush.

Phil is in control of his hooked carp but he's aware that as the fish gets closer the big reed beds, right and left, could prove a problem. Once the fish is beaten, he'll really pile on the pressure.

" The fish in my lake seem very supicious of baits. Any tips? "

These days in your local tackle shop you can buy all manner of plastic imitation baits – pieces of sweetcorn or maggots are a good example. These are very buoyant and neutralise the weight of the hook. They can often have a huge impact on the number of bites, and therefore increase the number of fish you land. Don't be worried about putting just artificial baits on the hook. The fish won't mind the taste as long as they look like the real thing. Alternatively try mixing plastic imitation bates with the real thing – this will impart the smell of the real bait too.

Keep the net still and wait for the fish to be brought to it. Don't chase a fish with a net.

Focus on Carp

Throughout Europe and much of the rest of the world, the carp is quite definitely the first and foremost bait-caught quarry. They are big, they fight hard, they're generally good to look at and they are plentiful – the ideal quarry.

Personally, I think it's wrong to begin your fishing career with carp – certainly with the specialized techniques that carp fishing involves. In my opinion, you learn to float fish, to leger and to catch all types of species before you devote yourself to the long–stay sessions that a lot of carp fishing involves.

Whatever you decide to do, you will find that a lot of carp fishing is very technical and demands specialized gear. You can, of course, catch carp with all the simple, traditional techniques but carp fishermen have taken the sport to a new level of science. If you are really going to take carp fishing seriously, buy specialized books and magazines and to go to a specialized carp fishing shop. This isn't a cop out! It's just that the world of carp fishing is extremely complex – far more complex than I can get over here in a few hundred words. However, here are just a few pointers.

Your quarry Whatever fishing you are going to do, it's wise to study your quarry. Carp are one of the most cunning fish out there and they learn quickly from their mistakes. They can also grow to a great age – over 60 years – and they have long memories. You have, therefore, to take the carp itself very seriously. One of the nice things about carp fishing is that carp are frequently very visible, which in itself is exciting. Look for them on the surface in warm, still weather. You'll also see them amongst lilies and reed beds.

In the wild, carp tend to feed heavily on small invertebrates – bloodworm, daphnia, shrimps, beetles and tiny snails. The whole lake is a larder and so they rarely need anglers' baits unless the fish are heavily stocked in a relatively barren commercial fishery.

Carp have very acute eyesight, especially when close up to terminal rigs. They also have a great sense of smell, a discriminating sense of taste and very sensitive mouths. Their hearing is good and they can pick up the sound of a lead hitting the water from many, many metres off. Carp can detect any flaw in your bait or presentation and they're very clever, testing baits before swallowing or rejecting them.

There are some glorious varieties of carp now swimming in our waters. This is a variety of a fully-scaled ghost carp.

A very confident surface-feeding carp, preoccupied with surface titbits.

A lovely carp caught on a free-running rig.

Carp Knots

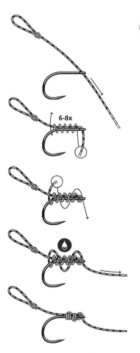

Knotless knot with hair

1 Tie a small loop near the end of your hook link.

2 Thread the other end through the hook eye. Wind the tag end (6-8 turns) towards the hook bend.

3 Wind it back two turns up the shank.

4 Pass the tag end through the hook eye in the same direction as before.

5 Moisten the knot and pull it tight.

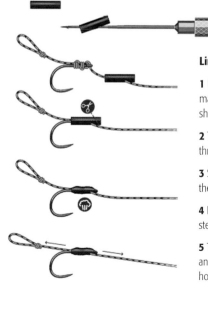

Line aligner

1 Using a baiting needle, make a hole in a piece of shrink tube.

2 Thread the hooklink through the hole.

3 Slide the shrink tube over the knotted hook and trim.

4 Heat the shrink tube using steam or hot water.

5 Trim the top of the tube at an angle matching the hooklink exiting the tubing.

Preparation Prepare very carefully for any carp fishing session. Choose your location meticulously. You will be spending a lot of time there and almost certainly putting in a lot of bait to attract the carp and keep them feeding in your area, so you need to be sure that you are correctly positioned. Boilies, various seeds and maybe even sweetcorn would probably make a suitable mix. You can get your mix to the required part of your swim by catapult, by throwing stick or by spod. If you have a boat, you can row to the area and bucket the mix over the side with complete accuracy.

Gear Rods, reels, lines, rigs and knots all must be 100 per cent reliable. Carp are big, powerful fish and head straight for snags. Any flaws will be instantly revealed.

Baits Although most carp fishing takes place with leads on the bottom, it's also possible to catch carp off the surface with floating baits, especially in the summer when the weather is warm and settled. Common floating baits are soaked dog biscuits, cat biscuits and plain old bread crust. It's a good idea to send free samples of these floating baits out on the wind to attract the fish but don't overfeed. Don't forget, also, that sometimes a big, single, floating bait can be the most effective weapon of all.

Hooks Often you will be able to fish with just a hook on the end of the line. Sometimes, though, a specially designed float helps to signal a take, particularly at range. Frequently the fish are wary of the line, however, so, if you can, disguise it by lying it over thick weed, lilies or in bays full of accumulated surface scum.

Hooks are a problem. A heavy hook pulls the bait down slightly lower than the natural loose feed around it. A large bait, such as a piece of floating crust or floating paste, will hide the hook to some degree, so the problem isn't as intense as it is with a small bait. If you are using small, floating particles, floating plastic imitations can be useful. Or you can use several of the particles on one hook, which makes it more buoyant and disguises it well. A hook can also be made buoyant by simply gluing a piece of polystyrene to the shank. Or you can use floating baits on a hair rig. Keep experimenting until you find the right method of attack.

Strikes With big baits like floating crusts don't be in too much of a hurry to strike. Wait until the line draws tight, as carp can sometimes take a floating bait between their lips and sink down without actually taking it into the mouth. A premature strike simply results in a spooked fish.

Jargon Buster

A **spod** is a large plastic container that is tied to the heavy line of a stout rod and packed full of bait. It is then cast out to the fishing area, where it upends and deposits the bait accurately. Spods can be used to carry boilies, particles and even ground bait.

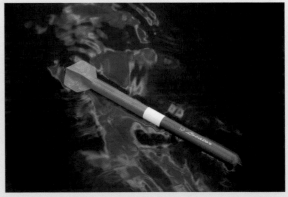

This is a marker float. You cast it out in the area that you have baited up so you know exactly where to put your hook bait.

Carp fishing The photographs and diagrams provide a basic guide to the rudiments of carp fishing. When you start out, don't make the rigs too complex. Advance stage by stage and don't move on until you are confident with the knowledge you have built up.

❝ *Carp are one of the most cunning fish and they learn quickly from their mistakes.* ❞

Not all carp runs take yards of line off the reel. Sometimes you will just notice a very delicate pick up and it pays to investigate closely.

Carp Rigs

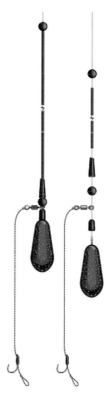

Free-running rig
This rig allows the fish to run with the minimal resistance.

Semi-fixed bolt rig
This rig holds the lead in place so the hook can prick the fish without causing it to bolt.

Safety inline lead
The safety inline system is probably the most commonly used bolt rig. Used on hard bottomed, weed-free waters, it allows the lead to detach itself when snagged. The rig tubing prevents tangles.

Helicopter rig
With its aerodynamic and anti-tangle properties, this is an excellent rig for extreme distances.

Fly Fishing

I love every type of fishing there is. But if I had to choose just one type for the rest of my life, it would be fly-fishing. Firstly the kit is just so simple: rod, reel, box of flies, bits and bobs in a vest and you're away. No messing about with baits or boxes or bags. So neat, so simple, everything can be kept in the boot of a car. And you can't deny that there is something inherently satisfying about catching a fish on the fly. Especially if that fly is imitating almost exactly what the fish is feeding upon. You see a sedge fly or a mayfly on the surface of the river and you cast out your imitation. It's taken by a fish that's fooled completely. How sexy is that!

YOU DON'T EVEN HAVE TO CATCH anything at all to have had a great day. The very act of casting a fly is something to savour. Good fly casting is a true physical skill. It's like kicking a football or executing a great golf swing. You can fish really well all day long when you're fly casting and enjoy every minute of it. The day is a success whether a fish comes along or not.

It's probably for this reason that women worldwide tend to gravitate towards fly–fishing. It's clean, it's elegant, it's fun and it's all–engrossing. When you're in the groove with a fly rod in your hand, you just don't think about anything else on earth.

Howard is an England International and you can see here he is perfectly equipped for any challenge the day might throw at him.

There was a time when fly–fishing was considered the sport of the rich. It's true, admittedly, that some of the very best salmon and trout waters around the world can be expensive, but these are the exception and not the norm. Today, on every continent, there are fly–fishing possibilities galore that don't cost much at all. In fact, if you take up fly–fishing in the sea, you'll find that it's free!

> *It's clean, it's elegant, it's fun and it's all-engrossing.*

Tim lowers his profile. There are some big fish feeding just beneath him and in crystal clear, shallow water he's making himself look small.

Tackle Shop

A lot of fly-fishing tackle these days is bought mail order or on the Internet, which is fine if you know exactly what you want. However, if you are unsure it is better to go to a traditional tackle shop and actually get the feel of the gear before making a purchase. Buy magazines to read the reviews and don't be afraid of asking anglers on the bank or fishery owners their opinions. Even if you start out by buying economy gear, this doesn't mean to say that it won't be very good and won't last you for many years. Rods and reels are now of a very high standard indeed, even when they are budget priced, so take care to buy something you really like and that you will want to use for years to come.

Rods If you are just choosing one rod to start with, then a 2.7m (9ft) or 1.9m (6½ft), 6/7–weight is about what you are looking for, certainly for nearly all trout and grayling work. You'd even find a rod like this is capable of coping with small summer salmon in tight situations. And 1.3–1.8kg (3–4lb) sea trout won't be too much for it either. Ideally, the rod will be tough, light and have a nice, easy casting action. Some rods, especially for long distance, are very fast in action and take some expertise to get used to. Look for nice whippings, good–quality, cork handles, top–quality line guides and, if possible, a carrying tube for protection. Rods with lifetime guarantees are now fairly common and really worth hunting for.

As your career progresses, you might find that

A nine-foot, seven-weight rod is a really good tool to start off with.

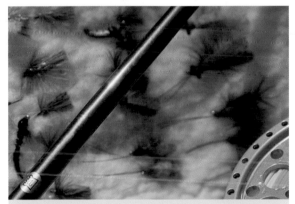

If you're fishing smaller rivers and streams, a lighter rod – perhaps a three or four-weight – is going to be more applicable.

you want to move onto very small streams. To tempt really wily trout and grayling in crystal-clear water you might soon start using a 2.1m (7ft), 3-weight, perhaps. Alternatively you might move onto big reservoirs where a 3m (10ft) rod will give you extra casting distance. Or perhaps you will take up double-handed salmon fishing and gravitate towards 4m (13ft), 4.3m (14ft) or even 4.5m (15ft) 12-weight rods.

> 66 *Take care to buy something you really like and that you will want to use for years to come.* 99

Weights And what's all this weight business? Well I could give you detailed explanations but, in essence, it's broadly the way we describe the power of the rod and the weight of line that it casts best with. A 3–weight rod, therefore, hasn't got as much power as a 10–weight rod. With a 3–weight rod you buy a light 3–weight line and with a 10–weight rod you might buy a much heavier, thicker 10–weight line.

Reels These days, even cheap reels should be light, have a reasonable clutch system and be very reliable. Let's assume that you are starting with the 2.9m (9½ft), 6-weight outfit: you'll want a reel to match, one that can take a 6– or 7–weight line with ease, along with perhaps 100m (300ft) of backing. You probably won't need this much to start with, but you'll be surprised how much line a big rainbow trout can run off.

Always make sure your reels are filled to the rim. This makes the retrieve a lot faster.

Modern reels are supremely well engineered, so look after them. Make sure grit doesn't get into the workings.

A super mayfly has landed on your reel. Now there's a clue for what artificial to put on your tippet!

Jeremy Lucas, an England International, is an ideal study in heron-like concentration.

As you progress, you might well move to tiny reels on that 3-weight rod of yours, or larger reels for reservoir fishing or attempts after salmon. For reservoir work, it is useful to buy a reel with different spools, or cassettes. This allows you to have different types of line on a number of different cassettes, enabling you to switch over quickly. 'Arbour' is a word in common use these days. Large arbour simply means that the spool of the reel is very wide. Mid-arbour would be my choice. With mid-arbour reels you tend to find that the line sits nicely and doesn't come off like loops of barbed wire.

Lines Fly lines are one item where it does not pay to economize. A good line will cast like a dream, whereas a poorer line will always be a struggle. There are so many fly lines on the market that choosing can seem difficult. As a beginner, you'll probably just need a floating line and a medium sinking line in case you want to get your fly down deeper in the water column. There are many different types of line, some sinking very fast indeed for deep-water work in cold or hot weather. Don't worry about these yet because they are very specialized.

It's the same with the design of the line. Some have slightly different tapers and profiles for different jobs. The most common are double taper or weight-forward. The latter is now the best-selling line on the market and is probably your best choice for quick, easy distance casting. All weight-forward means is that the heaviest and thickest part of the line is at the front so that it shoots out better when you cast. It's good to have a nice visible colour but one that isn't too glaring. I like light green or even sky blue. You need to see the line a lot of the time so that you can watch for it to move, indicating a taking fish.

Jargon Buster

Double taper is the term for one of the most common types of fly line. It means that the line tapers towards each end, with the thickest part of the line in the middle. This means that you can reverse a line on the reel if one end of it begins to wear out.

Accessories It's not a bad idea to buy one of the big mail order catalogues and have a browse through to see what knick-knacks the fly angler needs. Clippers, hook sharpeners, forceps and scissors are all useful. You might need oils or powders to make your tippets and flies either float or sink. Strike indicators – pieces of plastic that stick on the leader to show bites – are also useful in certain tricky situations when they are allowed. And you will certainly need a fly box for the all-important flies.

Forceps are an essential tool. You'll need them to flatten down barbs on hooks and then to remove hooks from the fish's mouth.

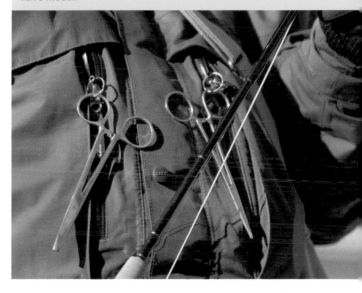

Fly tying is an art in itself. There are thousands of fly tyers around the world who don't even go fishing!

Leaders On the end of your fly line you will attach a nylon leader. You can make these up yourself but, early on, it's probably best to buy them machine tapered and ready to go. A tapered leader is important because it helps you present your fly better. Match the end of the leader, or the tippet, with the size of fly you are using and the size of fish you're pursuing. For example, if you're after small trout with tiny flies you want a very fine tippet indeed. If you're after big salmon in a heavy river, you won't be going less than 20- or 25-lb breaking strain. Balance is everything.

Flies If you look in a catalogue or go into a tackle shop you will see an alarming number of flies and it is easy to panic. Don't. As you start out there are three major types of fly to kick your selection off. Firstly, there are lures, large flies tied to imitate small fish or simply to attract the curiosity of a trout. They are quite heavy to cast and you generally work them back quite quickly towards you. White, black, green, yellow and orange are good starting colours. Lure fishing isn't the most intelligent side of fly-fishing but it certainly works, especially where the fish are stocked and not wild.

Up next are nymph imitations. Most trout and grayling spend most of their life feeding on nymphs of one type or another, and there are many anglers who never fish any other type of fly at all. Try to build up a collection of nymphs of different sizes, weights, colours and types. A good start is the pheasant tail. Gold head nymphs are also popular. Favourite colours are black, brown and olive green.

A dry fly is one that floats on the surface; they are very useful when you get to the river or lake and find the rings of rising trout everywhere. The most obvious example is the glorious mayfly. The real flies hatch in May and early June in the Northern Hemisphere and the trout go wild for them. But there are lots of other less obvious flies: CDCs are amongst my favourite dries, along with Adams, and I'd never go anywhere without some blue-winged olives. Almost as important as the patterns, though, is the size. It pays to stock up with mayflies as large as size 8 plus some little black gnats that might be tied on a size 18 or 20 hook.

If you're fishing wild, stony rivers, you might want some flashy wet flies like bloody butchers. These are very traditional; you cast them downriver and let them skip across the current. If you're fishing a lot of stillwaters, especially towards the end of the day, you might want a selection of buzzers. These imitate hatching midges and are fished just under the surface. When you're setting out, it's vital to ask the advice of fishery owners and managers everywhere. They'll recognize you as a beginner and should, if they're any good at all, advise you on the best patterns. Remember that everyone has their own favourite patterns and they tend to fish these with added confidence. And confidence is everything in fly-fishing.

> " *If you're fishing wild, stony rivers, you might want some flashy wet flies like bloody butchers.* "

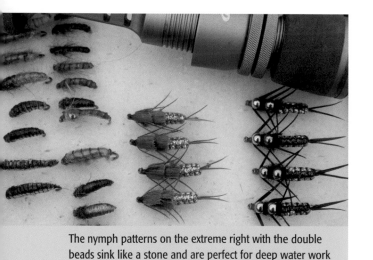

The nymph patterns on the extreme right with the double beads sink like a stone and are perfect for deep water work in fast currents.

Quite a mix of flies. An imitation ladybird would you believe! Even a wasp / bee pattern can have its uses.

The Fly Box

The following are the standard patterns that most anglers will always have with them.

Buzzer

Corixa

Shrimp

Czech Nymph

Pheasant Tail

Hackled Wet Fly

Winged Wet Fly-Butcher

Emerger

Parachute Fly

Dry Caddis

Dry Daddy-long-legs

Hackled Dry Fly

Mayfly-Green Drake

Winged Dry Fly-Greenwell

Salmon-Tube Fly

Salmon Double-Ally's

Salmon Single-Stoat's Tail

Salmon Treble-
Thunder & Lightning

Streamer Fly-Clouser

Muddler Minnow

Understanding Fly-Caught Fish

A quite spellbinding wild brown trout in close up. Catch a fish like this and you truly deserve to bask in its glory and your triumph. Try to return it in the pristine condition it enjoyed when you caught it. Photographing a fish like this in the water stops it damaging scales or fins and minimises stress.

Fly-fishing can be a tough one. A wild trout is one of the most easily spooked fish in any environment. Don't lack confidence but show caution. Any fish is catchable, providing you think about your approach and make as few mistakes as possible.

The hatch Watch what natural flies are about, either on the water or in the air. Inspect spiders' webs, for example, and see what insects are caught there. Look in the grass. Give it a kick and see what insects rise up when they are disturbed. Remember that fly–feeding fish like trout are quick to suss out a hatch and switch onto it. Match the hatch with a creation from your fly box and you're more than halfway there.

❝ *A wild trout is one of the most easily spooked fish in any environment.* ❞

Rise forms Learn to read rise forms. If the fish slashes at a fly in a splashy sort of way it could be that bigger flies are lifting off quickly and the fish are in a hurry to intercept them. If the rise is more discreet, the flies might be smaller, so there is less hurry.

A gorgeous rainbow trout. There isn't a more obliging fish than this.

Fish behaviour Learn to read how fish behave in the underwater currents. Watch how they might shift across the flow of water and look for a mouth opening. Watch how a fish will follow an escaping food item downriver and then flick back up to its original position. The more you recognize body behaviour, the more likely you are to see when a trout, for example, takes that fly of yours.

Colour If the size and the silhouette of your imitation matches the hatch, the colour isn't always that vital. If you go for dark, drab colours you will generally be okay – provided shape and silhouette are playing the game!

Shock tactics I've gone on about matching the hatch but don't ignore shock tactics if you're having problems. A big fly splashed in and worked fast can often trigger a violent response from very careful, wise fish.

Strikes A huge percentage of takes on artificial flies beneath the surface are never detected by the angler. A fish can sip an artificial nymph in and then blow it out in a millisecond. You've got to remain totally focused on your line and your leader. Strike at absolutely anything that looks out of the ordinary, however tiny the movement.

Dan is really working hard here, swirling his flies in deep, fast, oxygenated water.

Common Fly-Caught Fish

UK & Europe	Europe only
Brown Trout	Nase
Rainbow Trout	Asp
Grayling	Huchen
Salmon	
Sea Trout	**North America**
Pike	Cut-throat Trout
Perch	Steelhead
Rudd	Pacific Salmon
Bream	Chinook
	Sockeye
Mackerel (saltwater)	Chum
Sea Bass (saltwater)	Brown Trout
Pollock (saltwater)	Brook Trout
Mullet (saltwater)	Grayling
Sea Trout (saltwater)	Black Bass
	Char

Pauline is intent… the salmon are just in front of her in shallow, clear water. This is when single hook salmon flies play their part.

How to Cast

Casting a fly is an art, but it's actually fairly easy to master even though it looks quite complex. Much like riding a bicycle, good fly casting is all about technique, timing and balance. And furthermore, contrary to what many people think, good casting isn't particularly about physical strength; indeed, some of the best casters are women, children and slightly built men.

The basic roll cast The roll cast straightens an untidy line before you move into an overhead cast. It's also a very important cast in its own right, especially on small rivers or when there's no room to back cast because of tree cover. You can also use it for safety, especially in a boat when the weather is very windy. It's also the ideal cast to lift a sunken line out of the water.

2 When you get the rod to about 11 o'clock you should pause. You'll have a lot of line off the water and the rest will be slowly moving towards you.

3 Now sweep the rod smoothly back in a wide arc, round and up until your thumb is level with your right ear (or left ear, if you are left-handed), and the rod is pointing back to 2 o'clock. Pause again. The loop of line should have formed behind the rod looking much like a perfect 'D'.

4 Now it's time for the hit. Drive your thumb forward in a flicking movement as if you were swatting a fly on the wall just in front of you. Aim straight at the target and stop the rod sharply at 10 o'clock.

5 You'll find this movement should flick the line off the water and push it through the air towards the target, landing straight and true.

1 Start with the rod tip touching the water and then lift slowly but smoothly.

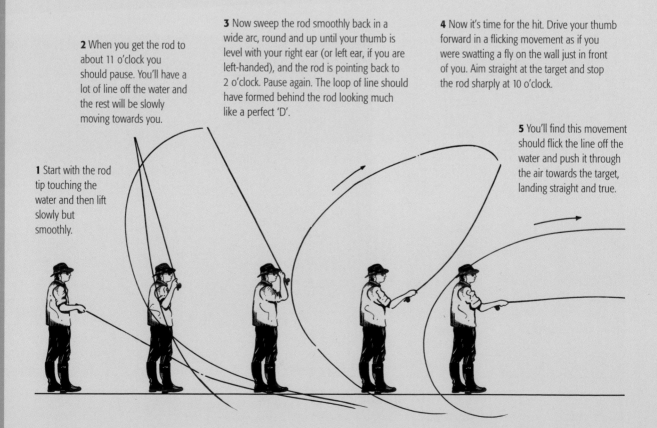

The overhead cast This is the main cast in the fly fisher's armoury, and you must learn it before going on to other techniques. It's simple – there are only three basic movements – the lift, the back cast and the forward cast. So don't be intimidated.

3 Your thumb should now be level with your right eye (or left eye if you are left-handed), with the rod pointing at about the 12 o'clock position. The inertia of the rod will have allowed it to go further back to about 11 o'clock. Don't let the rod go back further than this or the cast will fail.

4 You are now casting forward with your thumb driving the rod down. Stop at the 2 o'clock position in front of you. This movement feels like a tap with a small hammer or swatting a fly against a wall.

1 Start with the rod tip just touching the water and the line straight out.

2 Lift slightly with the forearm and accelerate gently.

5 The line is now flying out in front of you, arrowing to its desired position.

Don is a lovely caster to watch. Everything is precise and controlled and he puts out a very accurate line with a minimum of fuss. Notice how still he is. Although he's casting, no ripples are coming from him.

What Fly?

The contents of a trout's stomach are being analysed in this small bowl. Look how they are nearly all small, thin and blacky-brown. A real clue as to how your nymphs should look.

Don't get too hung up about this. In very many cases, a fish like a trout will take any fly that vaguely looks like a food item. For example, if a nymph is small, dark-coloured, in the water and can be seen, it stands a chance of being taken. Equally, if you are really stuck, on many stillwaters all you need to do is put on a big flashy lure, cast it out as far as you can and retrieve it at speed and you will get a take. Not always, but often enough to make life interesting.

HOWEVER, ALL THAT SAID, it still helps if you can match the flies that you're seeing as nearly as possible. The chances are that these will be what the trout are eating and your success rate will obviously increase. It's not difficult to recognize flies if you know what you're looking for.

Up-winged flies
The first important group of flies that makes up the bulk of the fish's diet is the up-winged flies, notably the olives and the mayflies. Up-winged flies can be recognized by their vertically positioned, graceful wings and long, delicate tails. They start off as nymphs, develop into duns

Mayfly

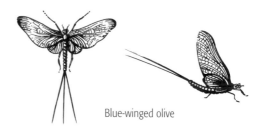

Blue-winged olive

and then transform into spinners. Mating takes place before the female lays her eggs on the water and dies. They are beautiful flies to look at and the fish love them.

Roof-winged flies
Next up are the roof-winged flies. These fold their wings across the body in much the same way as a roof on a house. The most obvious flies in this group are the sedges.

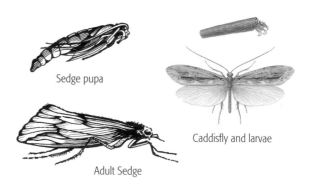

Sedge pupa

Adult Sedge

Caddisfly and larvae

Flat-winged flies Next we have the flat-winged flies. We're looking at hundreds of species from tiny midges to daddy-long-legs. All share common features: six legs, a pair of short wings and a well-segmented body. Most commonly, you've got the chironomids – buzzers as they are better known. The buzzer begins its life as a bloodworm before transforming into a pupa and finally hatching out into an adult midge.

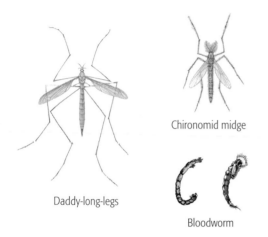

Daddy-long-legs

Chironomid midge

Bloodworm

Everything else Then you've got all the rest. For a start, there are terrestrial insects that land on still and running waters and are eaten. Alder flies, black gnats, hawthorn flies, reed smuts, moths and flying ants are all common foodstuffs. Then you've got crustaceans like freshwater shrimps and snails. Corixidae are known as water boatmen and look like small beetles. But remember, trout, in particular, will target anything that swims or ends up in the water – tadpoles, wasps, grasshoppers… if it's edible it will be eaten.

Even if you don't see the insect being eaten, the way the trout takes it often gives you some clues.

Water boatman

Slow rise Let's say the rise is a slow one. You see the head, the back, the fin and the tail, all in slow motion. This suggests a trout feeding on buzzers in the surface film. Fish your fly fractionally under the surface and retrieve it very, very slowly.

Boil on the surface Now, you simply see a boil on the surface but no sign of a fish. This is a trout taking food a few centimetres beneath the surface. It will probably be a nymph temporarily out of cover. Cover the rise as quickly as you can with a nymph pattern and you might well get a take as it sinks.

Audible rise Sometimes, in calm conditions, you actually hear a rise as well as seeing it. If you hear a sip, a suck or a slurp, this is probably a trout eating buzzers just beneath the surface or dry flies like sedges on the surface. Try a buzzer first. If that doesn't work, try a small dry fly.

Explosive splash Sometimes rises are explosive splashes that you just can't miss. These suggest trout feeding in a hurry on big food items that are moving fast. Perhaps this is a mayfly just about to take off into the air. Perhaps the fish is feeding on fry that are scattering and moving fast. Try a lure or a big dry fly until you unlock the secret.

❝ *Your success rate will increase if you can match the flies that you're seeing.* ❞

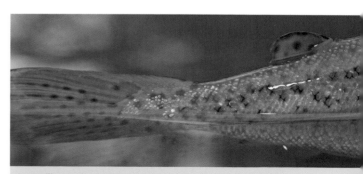

You will see rainbow trout in the surface film taking buzzers, especially when the water is very calm.

Detecting Takes

Stuart is watching intently as a brown trout approaches his nymph. If you can see the take, then you are 90 per cent of the way there.

A dear departed friend of mine, Mike, ran a local trout fishery. He was in no doubt whatsoever that anything up to 85 per cent of the takes achieved by his anglers went totally unnoticed. And it's true. A trout, a grayling especially, can sip in the fly and reject it without the angler reacting. So, if you fool a fish, how do you actually see the take? Of course, if you're stripping back the lure at speed there's no need to see anything, because there will be a huge thump on the end of the line. Equally, if you are using a big mayfly, you will see a nose come up and engulf it. No problems there. However, most takes happen underneath the surface and are very gentle. What do you do about these?

The line First and foremost, keep an eagle eye on your fly line and, if you are using a floating line, on the leader itself. It often pays to grease this so you can watch if it shoots forward or jabs under. Strike immediately either your leader or your line does anything unusual.

Strike indicators Where rules allow it, use strike indicators, especially for shy–biting fish like grayling. Also known as bungs, sight bobs and floats, there are many different forms of strike indicator. For example, you can use a very buoyant dry fly up the leader from a nymph. When the dry fly shoots under, the nymph has obviously been taken. Many American anglers like to use yarn, soaked in silicon and tied onto the line. It's very visible and it's very good in a gentle wind because it catches the breeze and drifts your nymph around on the stillwater. Indicators can also be made out of floating putty. This is a good

It's almost essential to use a strike indicator with grayling, a very quick biting fish.

option because you can vary the amount on the line instantly to make it more or less buoyant. You can also buy adjustable indicators. These are generally made of polystyrene and coloured yellow or orange for high visibility.

Using an indicator

Indicators don't always dive underneath the surface in a dramatic fashion. Sometimes they will just hold up against the current or move sideways. Or perhaps they will just stop in an unnatural fashion. Once again, if anything raises your suspicions raise the rod into, hopefully, a fish! And remember, if you're going to use indicators, it's a good idea to take a variety with you. Sometimes putty will work better than polystyrene. Other times yarn seems to do the trick. And if you're fishing a very low, very clear river for spooky fish, sometimes something natural tied onto the leader above a nymph will work well. A simple twig will often do the trick and look completely natural to a fish as it floats down the current towards them.

> ❝ *So, if you fool a fish, how do you actually see the take?* ❞

Observation

Use your eyes, especially with Polarizing glasses them over them! Stare hard into the water where you think your fly will be. Let's say you see a gleam 60–90cm (2–3 ft) under the surface. This is often a fish turning to take your fly as you retrieve it. A strike is always a good idea. Or perhaps you are targeting a fish you can actually see. You think your fly is close. Suddenly the fish's mouth opens and, if it's a trout, you might see a flash of white. Strike at once. Or perhaps the fish moves one way or another in the current. The chances are that it might be intercepting your fly. Again, strike at once. In fact, if anything untoward happens in the area around your fly, it's worth investigating.

Dead drifting

One of the high arts of fly-fishing is letting your fly dead drift in the current with no movement at all on the line from your retrieve. Even in stillwater you can bring the fly back very, very slowly so that it behaves exactly like a natural creature. The slower your fly moves, the more gently a fish will take it. This is why close observation is so essential. It's all part of your learning curve and if you halfway master it, you're on the way to becoming a very good fly-fisherman indeed.

Polaroid glasses are an essential part of the fly fisher's equipment. With these 'magic glasses' Pauline can see exactly what is happening under the surface film. Remember that when you're fly fishing, sight is just as important as feel. A peaked cap can also cut down on light from the sun and glare from the water.

Dry Fly Basics

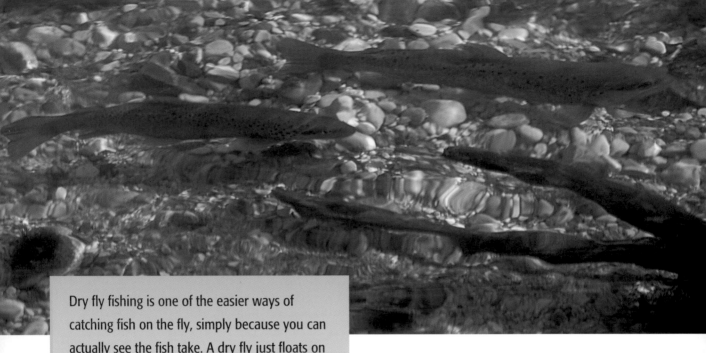

Dry fly fishing is one of the easier ways of catching fish on the fly, simply because you can actually see the fish take. A dry fly just floats on the water's surface and, hopefully, imitates hatching flies around it which are attracting the attention of the fish. So you tie on a fly that resembles the naturals, cast it into a place where you see fish rising and, with luck, they will be fooled into taking it. Job done. Or not. Of course, in the world of fishing, there will always be snags. So, how can you make your dry fly beginnings just that little bit more successful?

Matching your fly Fish can be a bit picky when it comes to taking a dry fly. With a nymph you're likely to get away with not being quite as accurate with your imitation. So look carefully at the size, colour and shape of flies that you see on the surface and try to replicate those as closely as you can from your box. Take with you a selection of Adams, along with CDCs, olives, sedge patterns and mayflies. These don't just hatch out in May

and June; you can sometimes see them later in the summer. Daddy–long–leg patterns are also a good idea in late summer and early autumn.

Floatant Always use a floatant of one make or another to keep your fly perky on the surface film. It pays to spray or dab this on your fingers rather than onto the fly itself. Now massage the floatant into the fibres of the fly.

Dave has caught a fine Indian carp on a big, bushy dry fly tied to represent the terrestrial flies falling from the trees above.

Tippet It's also a really good idea to make your tippet – that bit of line that leads to the fly – sink. You can buy material from a good tackle shop to do this. If your line floats right up to the fly, the fish will see it and become wary.

Casting Most dry fly fishing is done by casting upstream and retrieving line as the fly floats back downriver towards you. Approaching from behind the fish like this means that you are better concealed from the fish, which is facing upstream. If you are targeting a rising fish, try to cast your dry fly 90cm (3ft) or more upstream from it; not on its head, which will only alarm it. Retrieve your line at exactly the same pace as the river is flowing. You need to do this to avoid drag – that is, making the fly skate across the surface in an unnatural fashion.

Striking Let's say the excitingly unthinkable happens and a fish comes up to intercept your dry fly. It's all too easy in the thrill of the moment to strike too quickly and pull the fly out of the fish's mouth. Try to wait until the fly has been engulfed and the fish is turning down from the surface to eat it. This is particularly important if you are using a big dry fly like a mayfly. When using a mayfly, it's often a good idea to count to three before tightening.

Practice Good dry fly fishing is almost always entirely dependent on accurate casting. It's a great idea, therefore, to spend some time practising either on water or on your back lawn. This is not time wasted, I assure you.

Take your time When you get to a river or lake, it pays to spend time simply watching the water around you. Try to pick out individual fish, where they are lying and where they are rising. Look at the flies in the air and look at the flies on the water's surface. Have you got anything in your box that looks somewhat similar? Look, too, in spiders' webs. They will be catching what is most common around the waterside.

> " Dry fly fishing is one of the easier ways of catching fish on the fly. "

Watch what the water fowl are doing. When you see them feeding busily from the surface film, you'll know there's a hatch of flies.

Jeremy Lucas is dry fly fishing for grayling – an absorbing sport.

Nymph Basics

Let's say that you are on a river or stillwater and there are no trout showing on the surface. That doesn't mean that they are not feeding. In all probability they are, but only down deep, probably upon shrimps, snails, nymphs… anything that is small, dark and edible. This is why one of the best nymphs ever tied is a pheasant tail. It doesn't look much like anything but it's small, dark brown and could be mistaken for a score of underwater, juicy inhabitants.

Dan is fishing the nymph and watching for the slightest movement on his leader to indicate interest from a fish.

Find your fish The best and most exciting way of nymphing is to hunt out your fish. Watch it as it feeds. You will see it moving from side to side in the current, sometimes dropping down, sometimes rising up to intercept passing items. Sometimes it will even dig in the gravel to root out an insect it has seen.

Assess its depth Watch that trout carefully and work out how deep it is lying and how far upstream you will have to cast to make your nymph visible to it. If a trout is lying deep, you will have to use a heavier nymph and cast further upstream. If it's just under the surface, a lighter nymph will do. Don't worry too much about the pattern of nymph at this stage. As I've said, anything brown, or green or black will probably do; it's the size and the weight that are important.

When to strike You've made your cast, your nymph is dropping through the water column and approaching the trout that you've selected. Watch that fish carefully. In crystal–clear water you might even see your nymph and then see the fish move to intercept it. Mostly, you will have to strike on a hunch. What if the trout moves sharply right or left, up or down? Strike if you see the white flash of its open mouth. When you hit a fish like this, it's like magic, I tell you.

> ❝ *Anything brown, or green, or black will probably do; it's the size and weight that are important.* ❞

Czech nymphing Sometimes it is important to use a strike indicator (see pages 66–7). These are especially useful when fished with a team of two or even three nymphs. We often call this Czech nymphing. The idea is that you make a series of short casts upstream – it is a river technique essentially. You keep in direct touch with the team of nymphs under the strike indicator as the current moves them down in front of you and beneath you. Once they've gone a couple of metres, you simply lift the rod and cast the flies back upstream for a second run through. Keep the process going until you are quite sure there are no fish left in the area.

If you do fancy Czech nymphing, remember a 3m (10ft) rod gives you better control than a shorter one. Leaders should be 3–4m (10–12ft) in length for this technique. Once again, tippets don't always need to be too light. This is especially important if you're expecting big fish. Start again, with a tippet of 1.8–2.3kg (4–5lb) breaking strain.

The slow, deep water just away from the main flow is often a great place to drift your nymph.

Get out there! You can't hope to nymph fish effectively if you're always a landlubber.

A good nymph fisherman will work his rod constantly. It's often good to raise the rod high so you're lifting line from the water and just flicking that nymph in an impossible-to-resist fashion!

Buzzer Basics

Fishing with a buzzer is almost like fishing with a dry fly, insofar as you are very close to the surface indeed. However, with a buzzer, you are fractionally beneath. Imagine you are at a lake, especially in the evening, and you see fish, most commonly trout, bulging just under the surface. You will see the back of the fish and sometimes its dorsal and tail fins. Sometimes a head comes out. There's often a distinctive kissing sound. This is when fish are taking buzzers, the common term for hatching midges. They begin as bloodworms down in the silt. When they're ready to hatch, they come up through the water columns to the surface, where they struggle out of their pupal cases. They're now defenceless for just a few minutes and make a tasty meal for a passing fish. Buzzer fishing is thrilling and it's productive. How do you make the most of it?

❝ *Buzzer fishing is thrilling and it's productive.* ❞

Buzzers Make sure that you have a good range of buzzers with you. Sometimes trout can be very picky indeed and you will find that you need to change colour or size frequently. Have a good range of different colours, therefore, in hook sizes 10 to 14 or even 16.

Weight estimate It is important to estimate the weight of the fish that you are pursuing. It's a common fault to use tippets that are too light when you are buzzer fishing. On some of the Irish lakes, for example, people use tippets of 3.2kg or 3.6kg (7lb or 8lb) breaking strain. Probably, on most lakes, 1.8kg or 2.3kg (4lb or 5lb) breaking strain is about right. It is important to grease your tippet to within about 8–10cm (3–4in) of the buzzer. This means that the buzzer slips just under the surface but you can also watch your tippet for any sign of a take. Generally, it will shoot forwards 5–8cm (2–3in) across the surface of the water. Strike at once.

Casting Cast your buzzer as close as possible to the centre of the activity you are watching. It's a really good idea if you can pick out an individual fish and plot its course. Try to place the fly 90–120cm (3–4ft) ahead of where you think the fish is swimming to. Let the buzzer settle, tighten your line so you've got direct contact and watch like a hawk.

Fishing buzzers in the surface film calls for the tightest control and lightest of touches.

Tweaking It often pays to impart just a little bit of life to your buzzer. As you see a fish approaching, try just tweaking the buzzer 12mm (½in) at a time. This makes it rise and fall in a very appealing way.

Concentrate! Takes to the buzzer are often very gentle indeed, so you really do have to concentrate. That's also why it's a good idea to look for areas of the water that are especially calm. You're more likely to see that tippet twitch on stillwater than if there is a ripple.

Fish in crystal-clear water (like this rainbow trout) are sensitive to bank side movement.

Flat-winged flies

There are thousands of species of flat-winged flies, for example, houseflies, mosquitoes and crane flies. They're characterized by their six legs and their two flat, short wings. Many are land insects, but there are several hundred aquatic species as well. Buzzers or midges are among the most important for the fisherman. Buzzer fishing can be useful in almost any month of the year.

Adult Buzzer

The adult flies often sit on the water for a while where they are vulnerable to the fish. So, too, are the females when they return to the water's surface to lay their eggs. The adults can be imitated as well as the pupa. Try small Grey Dusters, for example.

Hatching Buzzer

Escaping the pupal case can be a drawn-out process and the hatching buzzer is very vulnerable to preying trout. The cast-off skins are sticky, and when there is a great deal of hatching activity you'll sometimes find them clinging to your fly line when you retrieve it.

The larvae

The larvae of the buzzer are commonly called bloodworm and they can be anything up to an inch long. You'll find them in the mud of the river or lake bed or among bottom vegetation. At this stage they're of little use to the fly fisherman, although coarse fish feed on them heavily, blowing up the bottom to get at the tasty morsels.

Pupae

Buzzers hatch generally from early spring onwards. At first, you'll find them hatching in the day, but as the season progresses they become more active towards evening. The pupae rise through the water but have quite a problem getting through the surface film. They hang there very exposed in the top layer before hatching and it's at this time that you'll see the distinctive, bulging rise forms.

Lure Basics

Lures are much bigger flies and they're tied with flashy colours and materials with a view to making a big splash in the water and attracting the attention of the fish. Lure fishing isn't one of the classic fly-fishing art forms like dry fly, but it is exciting, and effective – and sometimes it works when all other methods fail. Typical lures include boobies, dog nobblers, woolly buggers, cats whiskers and muddlers. Perhaps some of them imitate small fry, but perhaps most just look like a juicy meal of one sort or another!

Some fantastically weird and wonderful woolly flies here! Once they are wetted, they look a lot more streamlined and do become easier to cast.

Leaders Always fish with heavier leaders than usual when using a lure. You're retrieving fast and fish really hammer into them. They're not really examining the fly much, just hitting with force. Start with 3.2kg (7lb) or even 3.6kg (8lb) breaking strain.

Casting You begin by casting your fly as close as possible to where you think fish are lying, or to fish you can actually see. Sometimes fish are tearing around on the surface chasing small fry and this makes them definite lure targets. Pause for a few seconds while the fly sinks, then retrieve it back towards you. Vary that retrieve: sometimes short, sharp tugs and sometimes longer pulls. Retrieve fast. Retrieve slow. Keep experimenting until you find the key.

Speed up Very often trout, in particular, will pursue a lure along the surface. You'll often see the bow wave. It's tempting to slow your retrieve down, but in most cases it pays to speed it up and force the trout into making a decision. Bam! Thrilling stuff.

Change lures Make half a dozen casts with your first–choice lure. If nothing happens, move to your second lure, then your third lure and so on. Once a trout, especially, has seen a lure two or three times without taking it, the chances of it

> **"** *Lure fishing sometimes works when all other methods fail.* **"**

Roq is a master at hammering out a seriously big fly. Notice how he's all action putting a lot of body work into both the cast and the retrieve.

doing so in the future diminish fast. For this reason, too, it's often a good idea to keep moving along the bankside, providing there is space to do so. The more fresh fish that you cover, the better your chances of making contact.

Check the rules Remember to check the fishery rules. Some fishery owners put restrictions on the size of hook you are allowed to use. If you're not allowed to use any hook bigger than a size 10, you don't want to be caught using a muddler tied on a size 6!

To put out a big, heavy fly needs serious tackle. Forget your three and four-weight stuff for this approach.

Problem Busting

❝ I just can't seem to get the distance that people around me are achieving. On a big reservoir, surely that's ruining my chances? ❞

Firstly, let's think about your gear. Perhaps you are fishing too light. A lot of beginners set out with 5- or 6-weight outfits and there's no doubt that stepping up to an 8- or 9-weight on big stillwaters helps achieve those extra metres. Or perhaps your line is too light for your rod. It's not uncommon to see people using 7-weight rods with 5lb-weight lines, for example. You'd almost certainly find that a weight-forward line is going to give you extra distance, too.

Next up, of course, is your technique. Long distance casting is, to a degree, specialized work. Of course, with experience, your casting range will increase but it's never a bad idea to get proper, top-level tuition. In all probability, you will be taught how to haul and double haul – methods that put metres and metres on anybody's average cast. But it's difficult to learn these techniques on your own or from a book, so a day's top-class coaching will pay instant dividends. And don't forget to care for your line. If you wash it and grease it regularly you will find that you consistently achieve longer distances. If your line is dirty, grimy and coated with grit and sand you will never achieve what you should. Never skimp on your fly line. If you want distance, it's one of the most important items of your tackle.

But, finally, don't always despair if you're not casting those flies out at the sun. So many times it pays to keep on the move, get away from the crowd and approach the margins quietly and carefully. You will be amazed at the number of trout that come really close into the bank and like to feed there.

The rod has dropped too low, too early in the cast here with the result that the line is hitting the water violently. Keep that rod tip up until the cast is completed.

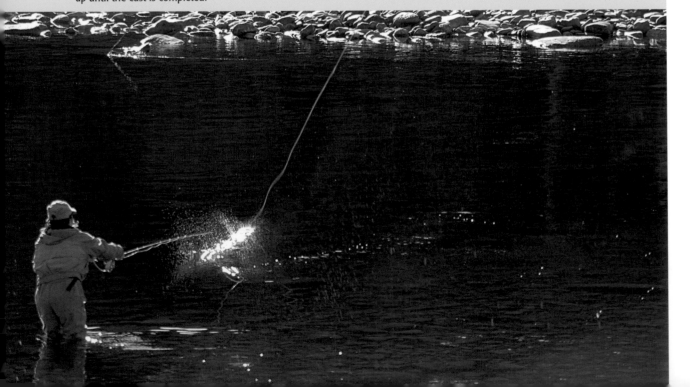

It often helps to work in tandem. Your partner can spot the fish for you and direct your cast.

❝ *I seem to get constant tangles and wind knots in my leader, especially in anything like a strong breeze.* ❞

Well, once again, it could be that tuition is for you. Perhaps you've picked up some bad habits which are finding you out when conditions are hard. Or, again, you could simply be trying too hard. Every time you put real muscle into a cast, the chances of a foul-up increase. Generally, it's better to rely on timing and rhythm to achieve distance. Perhaps, too, you're trying to run before you can walk. If you haven't been fly-fishing long, it's tempting to want to put out long lines all the time. Concentrate on getting out a nice, controlled line and work on your distance later. Perhaps, also, you are fishing too many flies. It's always tempting to fish two or three flies on a leader but sometimes, especially in a wind, you're better off with one. And don't forget, in a strong wind, even the most

experienced anglers will suffer from tangles sometimes, especially if the wind is from a difficult direction. If it is really seriously strong, try and fish with the wind behind you.

❝ *I can never decide on what leader length I should be aiming for.* ❞

Basically, leader length is all about the job in hand. For example, if you're fishing an average river with a 2.7m (9ft), 6-weight outfit, a leader of 2.5m, 2.7m, or 3m (8ft, 9ft or 10 ft) is probably about right. If you're fishing crystal-clear water for very spooky fish, some people would prefer a much longer leader – even 6m (20ft) or longer. A devil to cast, but it certainly outwits even the most nervy of fish. Alternatively, if you're fishing lures in March on a windswept reservoir, it is possible to get away with a leader not much more than 90–120cm (3–4ft) in length.

❝ How do I decide what strength of leader line to use ❞

It's probably fair to say that most people generally err on the light side when it comes to choosing a breaking strain. Okay, very fine leaders are sometimes needed with very spooky fish in very clear conditions but this is the exception rather than the rule. Even when you are buzzer fishing, it's often possible to use breaking strains of 2.7kg (6lb) or 3.6kg (8lb). This is especially the case with new material like copolymer and fluorocarbon. If you are in any doubt at all, go heavy rather than light, simply because if you do hook a fish, you want to land it.

❝ I've only got a floating line. Am I seriously minimizing my chances? ❞

To be honest, 80 per cent of my work is with a floating line and probably a higher percentage than that on rivers. However, if you are fishing a lot of stillwaters, there's no doubt you should equip yourself with a bigger range, at least an intermediate and a fast sinker. A lot of modern reel systems now feature cassettes – spare spools really, which are relatively cheap and quick to change over. You will find that this type of system gives you a lot more flexibility to cope with different conditions. If the fish are down deep, it's pointless to fish on the surface or vice versa.

Hooked! It's at high-impact moments like this that an overly light leader can be found seriously wanting.

❝ I'm used to fishing small, commercial fisheries but I realize that I ought to be a bit more pioneering. The trouble is big reservoirs and lakes really frighten me. ❞

Understandably! Big waters can be frightening at first, but the rules are the same for big waters as they are for small ones. Firstly, watch for fish. I know that sounds daft, but rising fish always give you a head start! If you don't see any fish, look for the anglers! In all probability, the locals will know exactly the best locations and they will head unerringly for them. Don't crowd them, but it's stupid not to use local knowledge when it is there for you. Failing all this, it pays to keep on the move. Travel light and after just two or three casts move 10–15m (30–50ft) down the bank. Keep going and keep going until you hit fish. Sometimes, on big waters, you might fish 4–6km (3–4 miles) during the course of a day. Obviously, it also pays to look for features. These might be islands, bars and weed beds, anything that breaks the water up. And don't forget, most reservoirs now have professional guides operating on them. These guys will really know their stuff and provide a short cut to getting to know a large water.

Big waters often hold surprises. Not all fly fishermen appreciate perch but they're fantastic fish readily caught on the fly.

❝ Wherever I go, anglers seem to be sporting fishing vests. ❞

And for good reason. You can carry just about everything you need in a well-designed vest. You'll probably have your forceps, line clips and even a thermometer, perhaps on retractable cords. There'll be room for your fly boxes, tippet material, dry fly floatant, a priest perhaps – everything you're going to need for an average day out. The great thing is you can take your vest off at the end of the day, sling it in the boot of the car and know it's waiting for you the next time you're going out. You'll find your fishing vest soon becomes an invaluable part of your fly-fishing experience, so it pays to get a good vest from the word go. Make sure the fit is really comfortable because you'll be wearing it for anything up to 10 – 12 hours a day. It is particularly important that the neck and the shoulders are well-cushioned. You will often have quite a lot of weight in the vest and you don't want it rubbing there. A good vest needs to be showerproof, at the very least, because it's going to have some weather thrown at it.

John Horsey, a long time England International, knows the value of a well-stocked fishing vest.

Lure Fishing

Lure fishing is all about using artificial baits to fool predatory fish into accepting them as real. The more skilled you become, the more you will be able to deceive predators by imparting life into creations of wood, metal or plastic. This is the excitement of lure fishing. It's a real art form. It grips the imagination. A difficult fish? Well, you can try a different type of lure altogether, or a different model, a different size, a different colour or a different action. You can vary the retrieve. Perhaps a short burst. Perhaps a series of quick twitches. Then bang, wallop, the pike, perch or whatever is fooled.

LURE FISHING IS ABOUT IMAGINATION, detective work, knowledge of your gear, mobility and appreciation of the needs of your quarry. That's why it's such a popular form of fishing. Neither your mind nor your body are ever still. You're always thinking, looking, casting, retrieving, moving on to another area. This is fishing for the adventurous.

Lure fishing is an all-action game. You're covering the water, often walking many kilometres, casting to scores and scores of features around the lake or river. You're always thinking. You never fish mechanically when you are lure fishing – if you do, you won't catch much. So you will get back home both mentally and physically exhausted. No wonder lure fishing is one of the most popular branches of our sport.

Lure fishing is all about mobility, imagination and excitement. You've got to keep on the move, looking for a big predator that's likely to have a go at your lure. Experiment with deep-worked lures or lures that pop on the surface. Try to think like a fish. Always make your lure work attractively. Remember that a big predator is always on the lookout for an injured fish, an easy target. Remember, too, that most predators mount ambushes so look for fallen trees, old boathouses – anywhere that gives them a hiding place.

What a magnificent river to lure fish! Dan is on an Eastern European stream that is crystal clear. Look at the depth – even in eight and nine feet you can see the bottom. It's a tense moment. Dan has located two very large huchen, one of the rarest of all the salmonids species. He could be just seconds away from the fish of a lifetime.

This beautiful, lure-caught pike was taken on a cold winter's day and fought hard and deep. Notice how it is being unhooked in a large cradle that will keep it from harm on the bank.

Tackle Shop

The number of lures available on the market is quite bewildering. To start, simply select a rod and reel that you feel comfortable with and then move onto a basic selection of plugs, spinners, spoons and rubber baits. Once you've decided that lure fishing is really for you, you can begin to invest more money in building up your collection. Remember that how you work a lure is much more important than what the lure actually is. Don't feel under-gunned if you go out initially with just a dozen lures and find that you are fishing next to guys who have box loads. Having the kit doesn't necessarily imply the expertise!

❝ *Remember that how you work a lure is much more important than what the lure actually is.* ❞

Rod You can cast a lure out with almost any rod but you're better by far buying something specifically made for the purpose. That's because you are constantly casting when fishing lures, which can be very tiring if your rod is not light and well balanced. You don't want a rod that's too long, either – most lure rods are between 1.8m (6ft) and 2.7m (9ft) in length. Shorter rods are lighter, more manoeuvrable and more precise when it comes to casting accuracy. Check out the rod butts: if you're going to use a multiplier, a piston grip style handle is most useful. Line guides should be top quality because they see a lot of action.

Reels Most reels will do providing they are not too big and clumsy. A lot of anglers make the mistake of using a light lure rod with a reel that's too big. Balance the two and it will make for a nicer feel and more relaxed casting. Providing a fixed spool reel can take a hundred metres or so of 4.5kg (10lb) line; this will do for lighter lure fishing challenges. Obviously, if you're after bigger fish and need to use 9kg (20lb) line, you step up the size accordingly. If you're really into lure fishing, you will almost certainly want to use an American style bait caster or multiplier reel. These give great control and huge accuracy.

Line When you're lure fishing, the line takes a real battering. It's being cast and retrieved time and time again and is much more likely to be abraded on rocks than, say, when you are legering. Always, therefore, buy a good brand and change line regularly. Braid is always a really good option. It's very thin for its strength and also very limp. This means that it isn't springy and difficult to control, which helps your casting distance and accuracy. Be careful with your knots when you are using braid – instructions are generally given on the box.

A modern fixed spool reel is the most common choice for lure fishing in the twenty-first century. Make sure the clutch is set just right. You don't want it so slack that it gives line when you retrieve a big lure. Equally, it's got to be set loose enough so that line is given when a big predator takes and runs. Always balance the reel with the rod.

Lures come in all shapes and forms. This is a plastic bullhead imitation. It's very heavy. The idea is to work it along the bottom in amongst the stones, exactly where you find the bullhead in real life. Takes can be surprisingly gentle.

Wire traces These are almost essential for most lure fishing. Even if you're not after a species with teeth in the mouth – like a perch – there's always a chance that a more toothy predator like a pike will come along and bite through the nylon. The last thing you want is a fish with a lure in its mouth. Always choose good quality wire. You will find this doesn't curl or kink and its strength is more reliable.

Swivels You will need at least one swivel somewhere on your line. Without swivels, the line twists and soon becomes useless. And don't forget your lure will be attached to your wire trace by a snap link. Again, this has to be good quality, especially if you are fishing for big predators.

Plugs These are one of the world's favourite lures. They are generally made of wood, plastic or metal. Kick off with a few plugs that work at different levels. For example, it pays to buy some top–water plugs that work the water's surface and a few shallow divers for just underneath it. You will also need a few deep divers, which work at depths greater than 2m (6ft). You can buy them to work at 6–9m (20–30ft), but these are more specialized. With these three types of plug you're up and running. Buy a few different colours of each and a few different actions and you'll be able to chop and change on a normal session.

These shots were taken on an autumnal day, when one has to work hard to interest any fish. Constantly changing the size, colour and action of the plugs was the only way to arouse some occasional interest.

A rubber fish coloured to imitate any silver fish found around the world. That big tail and thin tail wrist provide the clue to the lure's success. On the retrieve, the rubber works exactly like the living creature. Notice, too, the single hook. Much easier for quick, humane release.

From the wounds on this jointed plug, you can see just how popular it's proven with predators in the past. It's literally got chunks bitten out of it! You'll find that all anglers have their favourite lures that they have total confidence in and, believe me, confidence is one of the factors that you've got to develop. Fish without confidence and you wont catch fish, simple as that.

Rubber lures Soft plastic lures are made of rubberized plastic and come in all sorts of shapes and sizes. They are meant to imitate small fish generally but also aquatic creatures like worms, lizards, grubs, toads and frogs. You can work a rubber lure in many different ways. You can retrieve it, jig it or let it sink to the bottom and just twitch it back. Many of these come with just a single hook, which is great for fish welfare.

Spoons These are made of shaped sheet metal. Their bright, shiny finish catches the sunlight and pulls predators in from many metres away. Most spoons are on the heavy side, which makes them ideal for seeking out deep-water features. It's a good idea to keep your spoons highly polished because they really do rely on their reflective qualities. Spoons are frequently overlooked in the pike-fishing world these days, although over the decades they have caught more than their fair share.

Spinners The spinner has an angled blade with a propeller mounted on the shaft. When you retrieve the spinner, water resistance makes the blade rotate and flash. Size, colour and vibration are all important, and it pays to buy a good variety. A bit of red wool on the shank of the tail-mounted hook often seems to attract predators – perch especially.

Everything else You will need a shoulder bag to carry your lures. A really good strong pair of pliers to remove big hooks from bony jaws is essential. If you're pike fishing, it's not a bad idea to buy a pair of protective gloves, which help to shield your hands from the sharpest of teeth. If you're fishing for big predators, long-nosed pliers and forceps are particularly useful.

Understanding Lure-Caught Fish

If you are using a spinner, a spoon or a plug made of plastic, metal, wood or rubber, you've got to work hard to make the predator think you are offering them a real fish. So you've got to know how the predator thinks.

Clear water To use lures effectively, you generally want relatively clear water. Remember that the predators are homing in on your lures largely through sight. That's why it can frequently be very good if the sun is shining. The sun will bounce off a big, flashing, silver lure in particular and attract the attention of fish from all over.

Cloudy water If the water is very cloudy, fish will have much more trouble seeing a small, relatively discreet lure. Try something big so it throws out huge vibrations. Sometimes lures have sound chambers filled with rattling ball bearings. They will draw fish in from big distances even when the lure itself is invisible. And choose lures that are vividly coloured. Bright orange is a real winner but try neon pink, for example, or even white. You're trying to find something that pulsates and screams out to the fish.

The predator All predators are moody. They tend to take their meals in infrequent but large amounts and then spend a lot of time digesting what they have swallowed. So, at times, you've just got to accept that predators aren't feeding. However, let's say that you're fishing a pike lake. Perhaps the day has started very slowly. Don't write it off. What might well be happening is that the big fish are on the prowl and the small fish know this and are lying low. So keep your optimism up. If the water seems dead it might just be the day that you catch that red–letter fish.

A fine, bristling perch. They're probably my favourite predator. They're beautiful, they're cunning and they fight well.

Cover Predators aren't spread around waters in a totally haphazard fashion like currants in a cake. Predators generally mount attacks by springing an ambush so you will mostly find them around cover. This can be natural – vegetation, rocks, bottom contours and reefs – or man–made – jetties, bridges and piers. The tighter and more accurately you cast to these features, the more likely you are to have success.

Using your lure A big, wild predator has fooled many enemies to get big! So it will be clever, easily spooked and smart enough to identify a lure if it's not being worked intelligently. Whatever type of lure you're using and whatever it's made of, you've really got to make it look real. Use your imagination. Work the lure in shallow, clear margins where you can watch the action. Remember that lures don't always have to be moving to attract fish. This is especially the case with floating lures. You can cast these out, watch them land and then leave them completely for up to a minute before twitching back.

Predators love hanging around islands. This is especially so when the water shelves deeply.

❝ *Whatever type of lure you're using and whatever it's made of, you've really got to make it look real.* ❞

Plateaux like this can attract a lot of prey fish during the spring and summer and well into the autumn. Big predators like pike come into shallow water frequently to hunt.

Common Lure-Caught Fish

UK and Europe	Europe
Pike	Asp
Perch	
Zander	**North America**
Catfish	Striped Bass
Salmon	Steelhead
Trout	Pacific Salmon
	Lake Trout
Bass (saltwater)	Black Bass
Pollock (saltwater)	Pike
Cod (saltwater)	Walleye
Mackerel (saltwater)	

Reading the Water

Okay. You've got to choose the right lure and work it at the right level in the right way but, perhaps most important of all, you've got to work it in the right place. And you've got to understand that predators aren't just scattered around a water willy-nilly. The two words to understand here are features and structure.

Ian is fishing a fabulous piece of water beneath the weir. It's full of boulders and gulleys that attract big fish.

> 66 *The two words to understand here are features and structure.* 99

Features These can be all manner of reeds and weed beds. Fallen trees and man–made structures such as bridges, boat jetties, discarded shopping trolleys and sunken boats are also important. See what I'm getting at? No water is as completely barren and bare as a bucket or washing–up bowl. Look carefully and everywhere you will see features that break up the water and give it variety. Features are important to predators like pike, perch or bass because they give them camouflage from which they can mount an ambush. And, when full, a predator can lie under a sunken tree or in deep weeds and let the prey digest.

Structure This basically means a change in the bottom features of the water. This might be a change in depth or even in the structure of the bed. We are also talking about any bankside features such as points, underwater plateaus, reefs, channels and islands. All these places are important signposts to finding your predatory fish.

Ian, again, is on the point where fast water is beginning to slow and deepen. Big fish territory indeed.

Locating features You can locate features with electronic aids such as fish finders but these are expensive. On smaller waters Polarized glasses and, ideally, a boat will tell you most of what you need to know. You can also plumb depths by the oldest method of all – with rod, line, a lead and a float.

Reconnoitring a new water If you are tackling a new water, it's a good idea to go there for a day and simply walk the banks looking carefully for features and structure. Don't be in too much of a rush to cast in your lure and start fishing. A bit of preparation can prove massively worthwhile. So what are you looking for? Undercut banks, springs perhaps, fallen trees definitely, large boulders, rocky points, steep ledges, deep holes, shallow gravel bars, backwaters, bridge pilings, creeks, coves, submerged road beds, sandy bays, bulrushes and lily pads. Perhaps your water is a reservoir covering a flooded valley. Drowned buildings are great holders of predators. So, too, are old hedges and tree stumps left exposed after the trunk was sawn.

Of course, there are many times indeed when predators – pike especially – are caught out in open water, often not far from the surface. Predators do patrol looking for food and they're not always at home close to features or structure. But, the fact remains that if you are new to a water and you want to catch and build up confidence, you look to the areas where the predators spend the vast majority of their time. Makes sense doesn't it?

Exploiting structures and features Of course, once you've found a feature or a structure, you've got to work out how best to exploit it. What's the optimum angle to cast? What cast will give your lure the longest, most critical exposure to a take? Can you cast through the middle of the feature perhaps – say through scattered weed beds? Can you use a floating lure over a sunken tree? Is the wind going to make casting difficult? Would you be better going to the other side of the river? What weight of lure are you going to use? If it is too heavy it might get caught up. If it's too light it might not work down deeply enough, especially along underwater contours. You might want a lure that works very slowly, which means you don't have to retrieve it quickly and pull it out of the danger zone.

John is fishing a perfect position. Points like this on any lake attract fish like a magnet. They also give you a huge amount of water to cover.

Never neglect reedy bays, especially if you're fishing for pike. They don't always hunt in bays like this but you'll find they lie there to digest meals.

Plug Fishing Basics

Your aim is to fool the predatory fish into thinking your plug is a real, living creature. So you've got to work it right: you've got to choose the right plug for the situation and you've got to cast it into the right sort of areas. Here are just a few tips to get you going.

Know your plug Learn how your plugs work. Drop them into clear water where you can retrieve them and analyse their action. Sometimes plugs work best retrieved fast, sometimes very slow. Sometimes they look good just hanging inert without you imparting any movement at all. Get to know your plugs like friends. Know how fast they sink. If the plug is buoyant, how quickly does it rise back to the surface when you stop the retrieve? All these aspects are critical to your success.

Visibility Make sure your plug is going to be seen. This is especially important if the water is at all murky. It's at times like this when neon orange plugs work well. Or try black – in very clear water, in bright sunlight, a black plug often out–fishes every other colour.

Size Perhaps you'll have to use a bigger plug, which will be more easily seen and will send out more vibrations through the water. Perhaps you will choose a plug that has a sound chamber in which ball bearings rattle, once again sending out alluring signals.

Depth Get your depths right. If the water is warm and shallow and it's a bright sunny day, you will find lots of predators close to the surface, so this is when a surface lure works best. But you'd be mad to use a surface lure in the middle of the winter when the water is freezing cold. That's when, in all probability, you've got to get down deep and work your plug close to the bottom. It's for this reason that it is important to have plugs that work at all manner of depths – from the surface to, say, 10m (30ft) or so down. There are many times when you just don't know where predators are lying and hunting, so then you've got to suck and see and try all the lures in your box until you meet up with them.

Lures come in all manners of forms and these are two interesting ones. The top one is made of foam and is meant to replicate a bullhead. The bottom lure consists of lead – to get it down – and a series of elastic bands. This is meant to represent a knot of spawning brook lampreys! Cunning eh?

Casting Keep it accurate. We've already talked about feature and structure (see pages 88–9). Now it is up to you to work your plugs as close as possible to these killing areas. A shorter rod – 2.1–2.4m (7–8ft) – will cast more accurately than a longer one. Learn to feather the line with your finger as it comes off the spool to slow the plug down. If you don't do this, in some situations the cast will overshoot and you will lose a plug in weed or woodwork. Make sure that your spool is well topped up with line because this makes casting easier and more accurate. Practise. The more casts you make, the more accurate you will become. Don't get frustrated if it seems difficult at first. This is a sporting skill to learn like any others.

Make a plan Work hard at your plug fishing. Look carefully at the plug you've just bought. Are the swivels and the hooks strong enough for the species you are after? If not, replace both swivels and hooks with stronger patterns. Test your knots. Sharpen your hooks to perfection. Work out your plan of attack in any given situation. Have a firm plan about where you're going to cast and how you're going to retrieve. Stick to your plan. It often pays to cast to exactly the same place three times. The first cast wakes the fish up. The second cast excites its interest in the plug. The third cast sees it hit. If you are convinced that an area has predators that aren't responding, stick with the area and give them a choice of plugs before moving on. Watch carefully for follows. It helps if you've got Polarizing glasses so you can see into the water at distance. If a fish follows and turns away, try it again. Try it a second time with a different plug and you might just flick the switch of success.

Varying size Changing the sizes can be critical. Sometimes only the biggest plugs will be accepted. These really make an impact and can excite an instant response. But there are other times when mini-plugs do the business. You wouldn't expect a 14kg (30lb) pike, for example, to hunt down a 5cm- (2in-) long plug but sometimes this happens. Until fish learn to talk, we'll never know their secrets.

> 66 *Choose the right plug for the situation and cast it into the right sort of areas.* 99

A surface fished plug can prove dynamite on shallower, warmer water. This looks like a mouse, perhaps, trying to escape.

Think carefully about your retrieve. Don't retrieve in a rhythmic, methodical fashion. Vary it with lots of stops, starts and spurts.

Rubber Lure Fishing Basics

Rubber lures are my personal favourites. Because I like them so much I have confidence in them, and this means most of my fishing these days is done with them. I've caught some cracking fish on rubbers, largely, I think, because their action is great and when a predator gets hold of them, they feel realistic. Another advantage is that you can fish many rubbers with a single hook. This makes unhooking much easier than when you use treble hooks – hooks with three points – and so it is kinder on the fish.

Casting As with any lure, it's important to cast accurately. With rubbers you are best fishing at closer range rather than far off. This is because you need total control over that rubber. It will often be taken on the drop, so all you will see is a bit of slack line. Also, rubbers are often simply sucked in, rather than grabbed with ferocity, so if you're fishing at 40–50m (130–165ft), you just won't feel the take at all. Many rubbers are best just jigged up and down a little, which you can only do when you're up close and personal! Remember, too, that many rubbers are best just fished static on the bottom. Often predators will take a minute or two to study them before coming in to attack.

Keeping contact with the lure I can't over-emphasize the importance of being in contact with your rubber lure. Species like bass and perch will often mouth the lure without moving off, so strike at any indication on your line. If the water is clear, try fishing shallows where you can actually see if the lure is taken. If the fish are investigating the rubber without taking, this is your cue to change the colour of the lure, its size or its shape. Rubber fishing is all about intense concentration. It also demands imagination and intelligence. A tiny twitch here, the lift of a rod tip,

Types of rubber Rubbers come in all shapes, sizes, colours and forms. You'll find almost any food form imitated – fish, worms, crabs, frogs, crayfish, sand eels, prawns, lizards and anything that wriggles or swims. This can be bewildering. My advice is to choose fish imitations first and then slowly build up your collection. Remember that each rubber lure is best worked in different ways. Take them to clear water where you can see how they work at their very best.

Notice the heavy lead head on this rubber lure. This will enable you to cast far, to fish deep water and to work heavy currents.

the giving of slack line… all these subtle movements can mean the difference between success and failure. Above all, you've got to believe in what you're doing. It's only if you've got confidence that success will flow.

Experiment Take chances with your rubbers. For example, fish a rubber worm up the side of an underwater rock face. Allow a rubber lure to sink to the bottom between two big boulders. Let it settle there for a minute before twitching it back to the surface. Cast a rubber frog onto a lily pad. Let it settle for a minute and then just twitch it slowly off the lip. You could see explosive action from a bass or a pike. Sometimes the most outlandish colours can work well. Don't be afraid of purples and pinks.

Concentration Rubber fishing is very tactile and a lot of success comes through the feelings in your fingertips. With most lure fishing, you are retrieving at a certain speed and you expect a good bang on the rod tip. It's not the same with rubbers. I've already stressed how gentle the take can be and you are always looking for the slightest of signs that you've outwitted a fish. This form of fishing is almost like nymph fishing with a fly rod. Lose concentration or contact for a split second and you could miss the fish of a lifetime. This is another reason why I love rubber lures: fish them properly and an eight-hour day by the waterside passes in an instant.

Two fine perch caught on small rubber jigs.

No wonder Neil looks happy again! A twenty pound plus pike taken on a rubber fish.

Freezing conditions! When it's as cold as this, work your rubber fish very slowly indeed. Predators won't want to be chasing when temperatures are down towards zero.

❝ Rubber fishing is very tactile and a lot of success comes through the feelings in your fingertips. ❞

Spoons and Spinners Basics

When it comes to lure fishing, spinners and spoons are the most traditional imitations, and they've been around for many years. This doesn't mean, however, they don't work. They do. In fact, sometimes, their effect can be devastating. As ever, there are basics to bear in mind.

John throws a big spinner out into a heavy river. He's aiming for the slack water around a big rock.

Line twist Spinners, in particular, can make your line a twisted nightmare if you don't use swivels. Swivels go a long way to counteracting the twisting of the line that the spinner imparts.

Spinners and spoons These work particularly well in sunny conditions and clear water. The sunlight catches the blade and reflects attractively through the water for long distances. For this reason, in sunny conditions, it's a good idea to fish with bright silver or gold blades. And keep them polished. The shinier your spinner or spoon, the more reflection it bounces out.

The retrieve As with all lures, it pays to vary your retrieve. Know how slowly you can work a spinner before it actually stops spinning! If you're bringing a spoon back, the slower you do it, the more light bounces off it as it travels. Sometimes predators will pick up a spoon that is simply lying on the bottom. I remember fishing with a Czech guy who was having huge success by simply inching a big spoon across a hard, stony riverbed. To me it looked hopelessly unrealistic, but not to the fish.

A big pike caught on a silver spoon worked very slowly indeed.

Sometimes a black dot can give the impression of an eye – a real trigger to a predator. Sometimes a slash of red will imitate the gills of a prey fish. All these small things can make a major difference.

Changing size and weight On any given session, it's probably a good idea to start with smaller spoons and spinners and then work up in size. Think about water colour. If the water is clear, silver is great. If it's coloured, a black blade will work well or, at least, a deep brass colour. Remember, too, if the water is coloured, a bigger blade or a larger spoon will give out more vibration. A heavy spinner or spoon will work deeper. If you're fishing shallow, you need to go for lighter, thinner metal and work the lure back faster towards you. Try occasionally ripping a spinner back through the surface zone so it sends up a trail of bubbles behind it. There are times when pike can't resist this effect.

Deceptive touches Jazz up your spinners and spoons. Often red wool tied round the hooks will give them an added attraction. You can also try putting a tail on a spinner – tinsel, strips of bacon rind, small plastic grubs and even maggots often work well. Look at the blade of your spinner.

Silver spoons Most species will take a small, silver spoon. Trout, char, salmon, pike, bass, perch, zander and even grayling will all go for the simple, silver spinner. They are a real bait for all seasons.

> **❝** *Spinners and spoons work particularly well in sunny conditions and clear water.* **❞**

Lures come in all shapes and sizes and sometimes even seemingly unfish-like lumps of metal can be shaped to flutter and twist through the water in a surprisingly lifelike fashion.

The spinning spoon-shaped blades on these lures create flashes and vibration in the water, which attract predators in from a good distance.

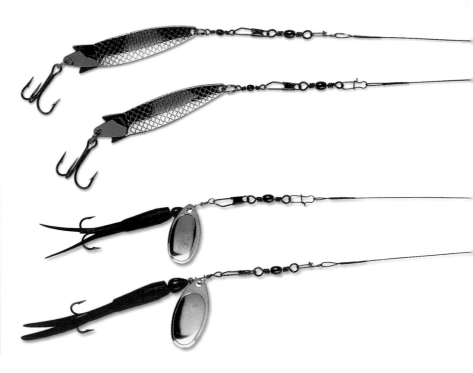

Lure Fishing Highlights

Black bass truly are a world favourite species. They don't grow massive – a five pounder is a good one in Europe and a ten pounder sensational anywhere in the world – but they are great to look at, very cunning and fight fantastically. What's more, you can catch them on fly, lure and bait. Those big mouths say a lot. These are fish with a healthy appetite and a gutsy approach to life.

Black Bass

I've adored my black bass fishing over the years in both the United States and Spain. I like taking them off the surface best of all. But to catch them in a feely–feely way, down deep on rubber lures is doubtless just as good. Let's just look at the basics of both.

On the top Whether you're casting a little surface–popping lure with a bait–casting outfit or on the fly, the rules are the same. Get that popper as close as you can to your feature. This might be a sunken tree. It might be a reed bed. It might be a branch sticking out of the water. It could be the bank itself. Whatever. Get it close.

Make the cast. Then let the popper rest. Don't move it for 30 to 40 seconds. Wait for the ripples of its landing to disappear entirely. If a bass doesn't come up, then give it a sharp, short pull. The popper should shriek out its presence and move no more than 15cm (6in) or so. Once more, leave it until the ripples have passed. Another short pull. Leave it. Two short pulls. Leave it.

It's important not to hurry bass. If they're proving difficult, it's tempting to speed up the retrieve and try and force them into an ill-considered attack. You're better off with a lure that you can move very slowly indeed. If you're fishing clear water, it really pays if you can see the action. Otherwise, feel the line for any delicate movement.

A big mouse lure like this can work for any predator, especially the black bass. Looked at from underneath it looks exactly like a mouse on the run! A lure like this is heavy to cast so make sure you've got a rod that's up to the job. If the bass attacks but doesn't take, move down to a smaller lure.

If a bass comes up don't be in too much of a hurry to strike. Wait until the fish engulfs the popper and turns down with it or you risk pulling it out of the fish's mouth. A huge number of fish are lost at this crucial moment.

Confidence in your popper is paramount. I've got my favourite. I can cast it perfectly on fly gear. It's 4–5cm– (1½–2in–) long. It's green and yellow and it pops like a firecracker. I don't think the colour is important but I guess the action and the size both are. Of course, I've had people around me fish with poppers two, three or even four times the size and they've raised fish all right, but I think when it comes to hooking them, I outscore nearly every time.

Down deep You can spin for bass or even use small plugs but rubbers are, in my opinion, the best of all. One reason is that bass love to take rubbers into their mouths to test them out and they're not immediately frightened by the feel of them. It's a great method. Bass can be the most critical of creatures, so if you fool them with a rubber imitation then you really deserve your fish.

Think about what you're trying to imitate. A crayfish? A lizard? A small fish? Even a huge dragonfly nymph? Think about what you've got on. What you've got to do is make your rubber behave as closely as possible to the living creature.

Hopefully, you can kick off in shallow, clear water and watch how your rubber is actually working. Does it look convincing to you? Does it look convincing to any bass that come along?

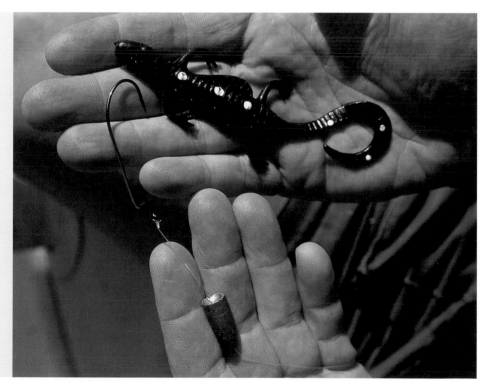

You see how inventive you can be with your rubber lures. Here we've got an imitation black rubber lizard which is about to be hooked up ready for a bass session. Notice, too, the lead above the hook which will slide down to the lizard's head and take it right down to the bottom rocks in deep water. A lure like this can be worked very slowly indeed, exactly as the bass like it.

It was a hot day and the glaring sun had sent the bass down deep. This small fish imitation, worked a good 20 feet under the boat, finally did the business for Raffa.

Perhaps you get a take. You can see it visually but also concentrate on what the line does, what you might feel on your fingertips. You need to build up this type of information for later on in the day when you might have to go deep down to find interest.

The sun's up. The air is bright and hot. The water is clear. The bass will be down deep, hiding amongst the bottom rocks. That's where you've now got to go. Now it's your line that tells you everything – when your lure hits bottom, how the rubber is working and when a fish is showing interest.

Remember a bass can take that rubber at any point during the cast, even as it is falling through the water down to the lake bed. Watch for the line checking or moving. Strike at once.

That rubber might be taken when it is lying static on the bottom. It might be taken when it's twitched. Whichever, don't be in a hurry to retrieve. Bass will often look at a rubber for

minutes, puzzled, trying to make up their minds. Sometimes four or five fish will gather round, as though daring each other to be the first to make a mistake. Crayfish, in particular, will hold their ground under this sort of pressure, just backing off centimetre by centimetre. Impart the same sort of movement to your rubber.

Lesson of the Amurs The Amur pike is one of the world's most glamorous species of predatory fish. It is almost identical to our own Esox lucius, the northern pike found in Europe and North America, with the exception of its colouring. The Amur sports black–brown spots on a tawny background. The fish looks like a leopard. It's beautiful. Ten years ago, I was fishing for them with an Eastern–European expert. He taught me that age–old lesson: you never know everything.

I always thought that spoons had to be retrieved slowly and steadily, somewhere in the water column. Not so. My friend cast out his lure and let it sink to the bottom. Only when it hit the bed did he twitch it slowly. He never reeled in more than 30cm (1ft) of line. And between retrieves he'd let the spoon lie inert on the bed for up to a minute at a time. It sounded crazy to me. But, at last, the biggest Amur of the trip was hooked. It came away, that's true, but the point had been proven.

Watch everybody around you. Even if you carry on fishing for another half century, you will always be able to learn something. And never discount any idea however foolish it might seem at first. There are always surprises in fishing.

❝ He taught me that age-old lesson: you never know everything. ❞

My great mate, Johnny Jensen, from Copenhagen, holds one of the rarest fish species in the world, an Amur pike. This is a stunning creature and well worth our journey of six thousand miles to find it.

Problem Busting

A really big fish picked up on a deep-worked lure and ready to be beached. A fish this large is not easily brought to a net so look for shallows where you can slide it out in the water.

" What is trolling and what do you catch doing it? "

Basically, trolling simply involves trailing one, two or three lures behind a boat as you motor or row along. The method is principally suited to large lochs or reservoirs where there is a lot of water to cover. This method is generally seen as fairly unadventurous and not very difficult. But there are complexities. For example, you've got to know your lures, how deep they work and at what speed they work best. It's probable nowadays that the modern angler will have an echo sounder on board and will be working his lures along specific contours of the lake's bed. Also, it can be hard, gruelling, even dangerous work managing the boat and three rods on a huge exposed water in the teeth of a force 6 gale. This is fishing at the cutting edge. All predatory fish can be caught trolling – pike, bass, perch, big trout, even Nile perch down in Egypt.

" What's the best way to transport lures, because mine always get into one big tangle? "

You can't simply lump all your lures into a bag and hope to retrieve them when you get to the waterside! One good tip is to buy plastic hook bonnets and fit those to your trebles. These mask all the points and cut out a great number of tangles. Alternatively, you can invest in one of the many types of lure wallet on the market. These have different polystyrene pages, as it were, and you hook your lures to them so you can carry them in an organized, tangle–free fashion. Also, it's

One of the many solutions to avoid the tangled lure syndrome! It doesn't cost much to buy a bucket and drill hook holes around the rim!

sometimes a good idea to take the hooks off your lures and carry them separately. Hookless lures won't tangle and it means that you can select the right hooks when you get to the venue and see how snaggy it is and how big the fish are. Remember that the hooks that come with your lure aren't always strong enough for every job in hand.

> ❝ I keep getting my lures stuck and losing them. This is expensive. ❞

Losing too many lures can be bankrupting! You're always going to lose some; that is the nature of the beast, especially as the good lure fisherman spends a lot of his time casting very close to

snags and obstructions. Sometimes a cast will go awry and sometimes you just won't know that the sunken tree has an extra branch beneath the surface.

However, a lot of losses can be avoided. For example, if you keep hitting bottom and losing lures in rocks, chances are your lure is too heavy, so go for a lighter one. Perhaps you are working your lure too slowly, so it's sinking to the bottom and getting caught up that way. Perhaps you're simply overcasting and getting tangled up in branches on the far bank. Take a bit of time out and practise your casting in a field, where you can gauge safely how much power to put into casts. Perhaps your line isn't strong enough. If it breaks too easily as you pull against weed, then you need to step up in strength.

" I fish a lot of clear waters and I can see fish coming short. "

This can be most frustrating. Just as you think a pike or a bass is about to pounce on your lure it will turn away in a boil of water. Well... firstly, it's always tempting to slow down your rate of retrieve when you see a predator following your lure. In fact, what mostly works is speeding up the retrieve. This might be difficult and you might feel you haven't got enough water before the lure hits the bank, but it might force the fish into an instant decision. A lot of this is about your retrieval. Keep varying the retrieve. Fast. Slow. Try to fool the fish into thinking your lure is real. Obviously, this is more difficult the clearer the water becomes. Once a predator has seen a particular lure once or twice and refused it, it is unlikely to come to it again. But you know where the fish is and it's an easy job to keep trying it with different patterns. At least if you're seeing fish, you know they're interested and you know you're fishing the right places. It's up to you to find the key that unlocks the door to success.

" I sometimes use my lures in the sea for bass and so on. But they keep getting rusted up. "

Lures are expensive and you've got to look after them. If you're using them in the sea, you need to wash them very thoroughly in warm fresh water once you get them home, otherwise rust will corrode the hooks, split rings and the metal itself. The worse thing you can do is to put lures still damp with sea water into boxes and forget all about them. When you open them up again you will just find a big, rusting mass inside. Whether you are fishing salt or fresh water, it's a good idea to let your lures dry out at home after a session. A few hours at room temperature will dry off any moisture. It's also a good idea to keep your expensive lures indoors, under a bed perhaps, rather than outside in some damp garden shed. Just make sure the dog doesn't get at them!

Fantastic lure water. Look at the big island. A lot of calm water on the left hand bank. Perfect. Then that small island beneath offers loads of possibilities.

Take antiseptic and sticking plasters with you on pike fishing expedition, just in case you get cut.

You won't see a more stunning pike than this. Beautiful shape. Gorgeous colouring. Pristine fins and scales.

> 66 *I always seem to have unhooking problems when it comes to getting my lures out of the mouths of pike in particular.* 99

This isn't an unusual problem. Many beginners, quite understandably, are very wary of pike and that big array of sharp teeth. The first lesson is not to be afraid of the pike. You can get protective gloves, which take a lot of the pain out of the unhooking process, I can tell you. In fact, make sure that you are properly equipped in general. An unhooking mat is great for laying your pike upon. I've already mentioned gloves. Then you need some really good, strong forceps. Sometimes it's not easy to get a hook out of that bony jaw. But this is where barbless hooks come in so usefully. You're not going to lose any more fish by using barbless; all you are doing is making it kinder on your quarry. You'll find barbless hooks slip out so much more easily. And, of course, if you get hooked up yourself the same applies. Use barbless and you'll cut out at least one trip to hospital during your fishing life! Whilst we are on the subject of hooks, do you really need trebles? Most lures come fitted with trebles, but often single or double hooks will do just as well, and they're

obviously a lot easier to remove. Many plugs, also, come fitted with anything up to three sets of trebles. Do you need that much hardware? Perhaps you can get away with three singles or a couple of doubles. And don't forget that the more pike you catch and the more fish you unhook, the greater your experience will become. You'll soon get the hang of it if you give yourself a chance.

> 66 *I'm told that clear water and sunny conditions are no good for lure fishing.* 99

This is not always the case. Out in India, for example, the guides insist you only use lures in the early afternoon when the sun is at its highest. The reasoning behind this is that the silver spoons and spinners really reflect the bright light and catch the attention of the fish. And it's the same all over the world. If you are using silver and gold lures, bright sunlight can be fantastic. However, bright conditions do often send fish down deep and so frequently you've got to work lures in the deeper holes in these conditions. One last tip is to use all–black lures in bright, clear water. For some reason, members of the trout family, in particular, adore these.

Sea Fishing

The world of sea fishing has really exploded in the last 30 years since I was a boy. In those days, in northern Europe at least, sea fishing tended to be carried out from the beach, often in the winter, generally for cod or whiting. There'd be some summer fishing, too, for flatfish and, of course, a lot of people went out on boats to make huge hauls of fish around wrecks. And that was pretty much about it. The revolution began in the 1960s and 1970s, when more enterprising skippers took light boats out to fish for species like tope and skate on comparatively light gear. Suddenly sea fishing became sporting and skilful and more people sat up and began to take notice.

TODAY, SEA FISHING MEANS a score of different things to different people. It might be fishing for striper bass on the coast of America. It might be fishing for sea bass around the shores of Europe. It might be hunting mullet in the marshes. It might be fishing for wrasse or pollock close in off the rocks. Or it might be using fly tackle, a method that is becoming increasingly popular off the shores of America and northern Europe. Most exciting of all are the huge strides that have been made in the last 20 years in fly-fishing the more exotic locations like the Bahamas, Cuba, Venezuela, the Maldives and the Seychelles… to name just a handful of locations. Fishing the flats for such flamboyant species as bonefish, milkfish, permit, barracuda and tarpon is the new rock 'n' roll of sea fishing. It's as far from the sport of the cod fisher 50 years ago as can conceivably be imagined.

And, of course, there's big game fishing in the sea. This isn't new. Zane Grey, for example, caught enormous marlin off New Zealand's north coast way, way over half a century ago. But, today, there are operations all over the world for fishing tuna, marlin, sailfish, billfish… you name it, it's possible to do. I have even perked for halibut off the shores of Greenland, where the water is 200 metres deep just a stone's throw from the glacier. It's not particularly skilful but the scenery is mind-blowing and the fish are awesome.

It's not all change, however. There are still men who fish the coasts of Europe in winter storms hoping for a codling. And there are still boats going out to catch fish off the wrecks. In short, whatever you want from the sea, the sea can provide. However, as a beginner, you are unlikely to get the opportunity to strike into a marlin! This short section cannot cover the more exotic branches of the sport, but it will point you in the direction of some of the most accessible sea fishing as I view it. We will look at the progress you can make in a much more modest fashion.

Do not be frightened by the scale of the sea. Although it is much easier to read the features of a small lake or river, you don't need to be overawed. Remember, just like in freshwater, the fish will always flock to certain, easily identifiable features. However, don't underestimate the sea either. Take special care if you are in a boat and always go out with people who are experienced. Make sure you know the timing, height and size of the tides. Always remember that you can be cut off by rising water. Never put yourself at risk. Always take advice from experienced locals. If at all possible, get taken out by them for at least your first half dozen trips. The sea is cruel and unpredictable, and whilst its charms and its gifts are immense, you've got to bear the dangers well in mind.

Here I am fishing amongst the ice floes in western Greenland for halibut. The idea is to lower a huge perk – essentially a metal bar with hooks on – hundreds of feet down towards the bottom where the big fish live.

Purpose built saltwater gear like this can pay dividends. You can be confident that the reel won't rust and that the rod fittings won't jam.

Harbours like this are excellent for many inshore species like bass and mullet.

Tackle Shop

Howard and Juan discuss the right fly for a Spanish sea bass. Notice the use of breathable waders and wading jackets – staying dry all day long will considerably enhance your fishing experience.

You are new to fishing so I'm not going to suggest that you set out and buy a complete new angling outfit for salt work, unless that is going to be your sole pursuit in the sport. If you go out with a charter skipper wrecking, he will often be able to hire you gear for the day. You can see if you like the experience and if you want to invest in tackle yourself. This is probably a wise move rather forking out and then finding you might have made a mistake.

IF IT'S BEACH CASTING that you are keen on, then all I can say is that you should choose your beach caster with care. Beach casters aren't all alike. Some are designed for smooth ground, others for rocky ground and so on. Be quite sure about the type of beach that you will be fishing from and make sure the rod you invest in is suitable. You will almost surely need a multiplier reel to go with your beach caster. My advice to you is to practise casting on a local playing field rather than making your first forays at night on some storm-tossed beach. If you're going to have problems and bird nests, best do it in the daytime so that tangles can be rectified.

A lot of modern saltwater fishing can be tackled with the sort of freshwater gear we have already discussed. This means, obviously, that expense is saved. What you've got to be careful of, though, is the element of the salt. If you take a spinning rod, for example, or fly gear that you normally use in freshwater to the seaside, you've got to make sure you wash it in freshwater very, very thoroughly upon your return. The same goes for flies, fly boxes and spinners. All these valuable items will corrode if you just let them sit in damp, salty conditions.

Let's look, then, at some of the sea opportunities open to you that can be tackled with gear you might already have.

Neil has spied a pod of feeding mullet in the crystal water twenty yards away from him. The tide is just on the flow and there'll be more fish coming in. A heart-stopping moment.

European bass You can walk the shore casting spinners, spoons and plugs with the rod that you would use for pike fishing. A 6.8kg (15lb) or 9kg (20lb) line should prove sufficient. You will find that you will be able to cast a heavy plug 60–70m (200–230ft), easily covering the sort of territory that bass enjoy. If they're feeding close, you will find that an 8-weight fly outfit should punch out a good enough line to make them a feasible proposition. If you want to fish bait – crab or worms, for example – heavy carp gear should prove more than adequate. I've often used a 1kg (2½lb) test curve carp rod, 6.8kg (15lb) line and a size 2 hook with a lugworm attached for bass of well over 3.5kg (8lb) in weight.

Mullet A 7- or 8-weight fly outfit will be perfect, casting the small goldhead nymphs that can often drive mullet wild. Alternatively, if you're fishing harbours for them with bread flake, for example, then a strongish float rod or Avon type rod will do very nicely. Team this up with 2.3kg (5lb) or 2.7kg (6lb) line and you should be able to tame the biggest mullet in the sea.

Other types of fish Try wrasse fishing off the rocks with your freshwater float gear. Try fishing for flatfish close in with a quiver tip rod. Try for pollock off deep, rocky ledges with either fly gear or spinning tackle. You'll find they dive furiously. Try fishing for mackerel with a fly-fished lure, much like you would rainbow trout. You'll find they fight three times as hard.

Exotic fish When exploring the shallow, warm seas of the world – the flats – for exotic species like bonefish and permit, you can adapt most freshwater rods and reels, providing you hose them down after use.

" *A lot of modern saltwater fishing can be tackled with freshwater gear.* "

The tide has flooded all the marshes and now there are mullet and bass feeding in water only a foot or so deep.

Understanding Sea Fish

The seas are huge and can be intimidating. Where on earth do you begin? After all, saltwater covers most of the planet and you've just got to look for clues.

Features Learn to watch for features that attract fish – piers, rocks, coral reefs, underwater vegetation. Walk your ground at low water and look for clues – rock formations, worm beds and areas rich in crabs and shellfish.

Tides Learn to read the tides. Look for areas where currents meet and mingle. Look for areas of tidal rips. You've got to make sense of the water fish live in. Remember that the sea is never still but is constantly on the move, pushed around by the tides and the winds.

> " *You've got to make sense of the water fish live in.* "

Signs of fish Though the sea is big, it will still reveal signs. Watch for feeding sea birds. They're probably picking small fish pushed towards the surface, driven by predators. Look for seals. You won't find them in any area that isn't rich in fish. Sometimes you will see small fish actually scattering – a sure sign of a predator behind them. Watch for fish in the shallows. Bass and mullet follow the tides in and, in the tropics, you'll see bonefish in water only centimetres deep.

Changing conditions Realize that sea fish have to be much more mobile than their freshwater cousins. Tides, currents, storms and weather changes all push them around their world. A good spot one week can change totally the next. If you've found fish then capitalize. Don't hang around hoping they will still be present a week or a month down the line. They could well be hundreds of kilometres away by then.

Approach Decide on your approach. Are you going to use bait, lure or fly? Which approach is most likely to entice the fish? Which approach is going to let you reach the fish in the first place? Which approach is going to give you most fun and satisfaction? Some fish – cod for example – are really only approachable on bait or lure, whereas a bass is open to all approaches.

Conservation And though the sea is big, this doesn't mean that there will always be loads of fish out there. Always fish with your conservation hat firmly on. Do you really need to eat that fish? Wouldn't you get more satisfaction seeing it swim away free in the surf?

The mudflats at low water offer a lot of clues to the inquisitive angler. You'll find all the contours exposed which will give you a really good idea of where the fish might be when the tide floods.

A creek like this will be full of fish once the tide begins to flow. Expect bass, mullet, flatfish and even sea trout.

Common Sea Fish

UK and Europe
Sea Bass
Mullet
Wrasse
Mackerel
Pollock
Cod
Whiting
Tope
Conga
Plaice
Dabs
Shark species

North America
Sailfish
Marlin
Striped Bass
Barracuda
Cod
Giant Trevally
Tarpon
Bonefish
Tuna
Jacks

When the tide fills these marsh head lagoons, you will find fish coming in to feed on worms, crab and shellfish.

Sea Bait Fishing

You can practise bait fishing in the sea in several different ways. The most traditional way is beach casting, a sport still enjoyed around the world.

Take care. Don't take risks with cliffs or slippery rocks. You don't want to be caught injured and on your own, in a dangerous situation with the tide beginning to turn.

Beach Casting

This is one of the rougher, tougher sides of fishing. It is frequently practised at night, in the winter, on storm–tossed beaches. In Europe, at least, targets will be cod, codling, haddock, flatfish, pollock or even bass.

Position and kit You'll often have to walk a long way across the rocks and beaches to get to the best positions. Your beach caster will need to be a tough piece of kit. Team it up with a multiplier. Baits will be lugworms, ragworms, crab or squid.

A shore fisherman like Tony often finds himself in more rugged, isolated places than any angler is ever likely to experience.

Tony is constantly looking for places where the shoreline and the tides work together to produce fabulous fish-holding areas.

Long casting This is frequently called for. This takes practise and timing. You are looking for specific marks – fish aren't scattered randomly across the shoreline. Rocks and weed attract fish but other species flock to clear, sandy bottoms. For your first two trips, go out with an experienced friend or join a club. This is fishing at the sharp end. Don't try it on your own.

Bites Just because the gear is outsized and you're fishing with big baits, don't always expect violent bites. Keep contact with your bait and watch that rod tip. Even a good cod can give the slightest of indications. Though it's on the heavy side, this remains a skilful type of fishing. And, even though your gear is heavy, you will be amazed at how hard some of these fish bite. Remember that frequently the tides are immensely strong; if a fish gets across the current you're in trouble, especially if the water is strewn with rocks, gulleys and tough weed.

One of Tony's secrets is to match the best baits with the season. His baits are always fresh and mounted with great care, to keep them secure during the cast and to withstand the pounding the sea gives them.

The shore is a great place to be. These are wild and lonely areas where you will be alone.

Float Fishing from the Shore

Now, we're looking at something completely different. You can use a beefy 3.6–4m (12–13ft) float rod, fixed spool reel and 3.6kg (8lb) line for many different species. Remember, as ever, to clean down your freshwater gear very carefully when you get it back home.

Mullet Look for mullet around harbours and marinas all across the world. It's in places like these that they become used to feeding on items thrown away by tourists, market traders and boat people. You'll find you can catch mullet in situations like this on bread flake, pinched on a size 12 hook and allowed to sink slowly under a float. Some mashed bread thrown around the float will help attract mullet to the area. Mind you, this can be very frustrating – frequently you will find that all of the free offerings are mopped up and only yours on the hook remains. Try using a smaller hook and a smaller piece of bread. Failing that, go to lighter line until you get success.

Neil is exploring an estuary at low water. He's looking in the mud for the distinctive grooved mark that mullet make as they sift for food there. This will give him a clue where to head for when the tide comes in and brings the fish. Doing your homework always pays dividends whatever form of fishing you are enjoying.

Bass If the sea's margins are coloured up because of wind or rain you can often hunt bass close in on worm or crab. You will find that your heavy carp gear will do for this type of approach. A 1kg (2½lb) test curve rod, fixed spool reel and 6.8kg (15lb) line should be adequate. Leads and size 4 hooks complete the job. Cast as far out as you can and let the bait roll round with the tide and the current. Keep close contact with your bait because a bass can easily pick it up, test it and eject it without you knowing a thing. Bites, generally, tend to be good pulls and you'll often pick decent fish up only 10m (30ft) from the shore.

Wrasse Let's say you've got a rocky coastline around you with deep water and good weed growth close in. This is perfect ground for the different wrasse species. Although most of these don't grow big, they're colourful, bold-biting and fight fantastically. The same sort of gear that you use for mullet is perfect. Bait with a small worm and let the float move in the current, in and out of the rocks and over the weed. Expect dramatic bites and heart-stirring battles as the wrasse dive again and again into the rocky gulleys.

Tarpon Let's look at a totally different end of the spectrum – bait fishing for tarpon in Florida! Ideally, you'll want to catch your tarpon on the fly but this isn't always feasible. Prawns and small fish frequently tempt these spooky silver kings. You need strong gear for this type of fishing with plenty of line of at least 9kg (20lb) breaking strain. Drift a dead fish in the current towards a feature – perhaps bridge buttresses, or alongside boats or off headlands.

Watch for tarpon on the move, perhaps ploughing into prey fish or coming clear of the water. Keep mobile. You'll need a guide and a boat for this type of game. You'll know a take when it comes. Strike hard and then listen to your boatman. He'll know how to conduct the fight and how to manoeuvre the boat. He'll know when to follow the fish and when you've got to clamp down and give it some power. Watch for the fish jumping; this is a critical moment. It often pays to lower the rod tip so your line to the fish isn't fatally tight. Remember to unhook these majestic fish – if you're lucky enough to bring one to the boat – in the water. Photograph? Perhaps you can pose with it in the shallows so the fish is always in its own environment.

Tarpon are truly the silver kings, not just off the Florida coast but through the warm waters of the world. Scintillating to look at, they are fascinating in their habits and when hooked, fight as fast and hard as any fish on the planet.

Sea Fishing on the Fly

A collection of different weight rods and reels can be vital if you are fishing at different depths around different features in rapidly changing weather conditions.

Remember, if you've got 6-, 7-, 8- or 9-weight freshwater fly-fishing gear, you can press it into service for many forms of coastal fly-fishing for species like bass, mullet and, further abroad, bonefish. I just need to impress on you the need to hose everything down carefully at night when you've finished. Get that salt out. Let's look at fly-fishing for bass – one of the great new sports over the past 20 years in Europe and America.

Gear It's great to have two different sets of gear here: a 6- or 7-weight with a floating line for calmer conditions and perhaps an 8-, 9- or even 10-weight and a sinking line for when conditions are more robust. Leaders need to be rugged because you're fishing in a tough environment. As for flies, there are endless patterns. Bass in the wild eat sand eels, elvers and tiny fish, so anything that is silvery, a couple of centimetres long and ripples enticingly is bound to be a good start. Clousers are a common pattern and are very effective. If you are fishing over rocks, crab patterns can also do well. If the water is relatively tranquil, try a surface-working popper. Bass don't always take a popper off the top but at least you can locate fish this way.

Conditions The best conditions for shoreline bass are calm ones. If there's a big wind, it makes casting difficult and it colours up the water so the bass can't see the fly. Clear water is always the best. Don't worry too much about the tide. In many places in Europe it's more important to get out early and stay out late. These are prime bass-feeding times. They can, of course, be caught in the day but those periods of low light are frequently more effective.

Features You've got to look for the features on your piece of shoreline. Bass love foraging amongst rocks and rough ground is great. Clean areas of sand and gravel aren't particularly bass-friendly. It's a good idea to walk your ground at low water and look for areas of rock pools, clumps of weed, fissures in the rocks, gulleys – anywhere that will trap items of food. Also investigate areas where freshwater streams run into the sea. Look for bass around groynes, breakwaters, rocky outcrops and sea defences. Pier footings are also a magnet.

Even when the tide comes in, the water here will be comparatively shallow, rarely more than three or four feet. This is an ideal depth for working the fly.

Technique You don't often have to cast far from the beach for bass because they do come in very close indeed. Far better to be accurate and target the places that look promising. Often you don't need to retrieve very vigorously either because the tides and currents move the fly for you in a realistic way. Try to keep close contact to the fly, though. Not all bass takes are volcanic!

Fishing from a boat I'm not including bass fishing from a boat in this particular section because, chances are, if you do go out in a boat it will be with an expert. If you are going out on a boat, it's likely you will need your heavier gear because often you've got to get down quite deep. You'll probably be fishing bigger flies, too, and remember that the open sea can be a very windy place indeed. That's why I advise your stronger outfit for this type of work.

❝ *Hose everything down carefully at night when you've finished. Get that salt out.* ❞

To get the better of sea bass, you have to be in there with them putting the fly where it counts. First-class waterproof clothing, a buoyancy aid, good balance and a bit of nerve are important ingredients.

When fishing for bass, spinning can be as effective as fly fishing, and you do cover ground a lot faster. Whichever method you use, be mindful of the fish you are taking. Be aware of size limits, and remember that bass take five years to mature, so just occasionally, try to limit yourself to only one for the pot.

Don't be tempted to skimp on the correct clothing in the tropics. Remember that safety always comes first.

Conservation The European bass is now a seriously protected fish. There are strict size limits imposed on the fish you can take for the table. The odd fish, now and again is fine for the kitchen, but restrict the numbers that you take over the season for the good of the species, please. We're sports fishermen; not fishmongers.

Bonefish on the Fly

Now for something very much more exotic – perhaps you're off to Florida, Cuba, Venezuela or the Seychelles. Wherever your location, this is a big commitment in terms of time and money. Do your homework well. The quieter and easier the flats (those beautiful areas of very shallow, warm, crystal-clear water), the less spooky the fish are likely to be. Make sure your clothing and sun protection are suitable. You'll need flat boots, too, to protect your feet from stingrays. Gear is vital.

Sea bass come in close to the shore to hunt the small fish and crabs that are hiding there. Flies should look, therefore, like small, vulnerable, tasty food items fluttering helplessly in the tide.

You'd never quite call a day on the flats hard work, but it can be gruelling. Perhaps the nicest time is when the sun is just beginning to sink and lose its glare, and the fish are beginning to feed particularly well.

A lot of people like to fish relatively light for bones but it's a good idea to have a heavier outfit in case a wind springs up. Your reel is particularly important. Bones can run a hundred metres when first hooked and so you've got to have a reliable clutch and plenty of backing. Check the knot that connects that backing with your fly line!

Spotting the fish

For the first few trips, at least, you've got to go out with a guide, whether you are walking the flats or fishing them by boat. The guide will know exactly the features that will attract bonefish. You're looking for the right combination of wind, tide, depths, food supplies and bottom make–up. He'll also be able to spot bonefish for you much more efficiently than you can at first. To you – and to me – bones are almost invisible, but guides learn to spot the slightest of clues. Pinpointing bonefish is absolutely essential before casting. The flats are huge places and you could cast a thousand times blind and not be near a fish.

❝ Pinpointing bonefish is absolutely essential before casting. ❞

Casting

When you're fishing and the guide has pointed out a bonefish to you, don't take your eyes off it. Keep it in your vision or the chances are that you will lose it altogether. Speed and accuracy are the two important elements when you're casting to a bonefish. Try to place the fly close to the fish, within its vision. It might be a crab or a shrimp pattern and it might be taken on the drop. Let it settle. Twitch it. Make it realistic. Look for the bone homing in. Strike and then all hell lets loose.

Fishing the flats successfully is all about hunting the prey. These are huge expanses of water, and you've got to move large distances quietly and carefully, always scanning the water for glimpses of fish.

Spinning in the Sea

Your ordinary freshwater spinning gear can prove a really exciting way of exploring the sea. Let's look at some of the options. All you will really need is a strongish spinning rod, say about 2.4–3m (8–10ft) in length, capable of casting around 40g (1lb) in weight. An ordinary fixed spool reel will do, equipped with line strength from 3.6–6.8kg (8–15lb). Once again, don't forget to wash down your gear carefully after you've used it in saltwater conditions. Don't pack it away unwashed in warm, unventilated conditions because it will corrode.

Mackerel One of the nicest ways of fishing the shoreline is to travel light with a selection of small, heavy, silver spinners in search of mackerel. Mackerel adore Mepps spinners. These are generally silver and come in weights 1 to 6. Six are the biggest and they're sometimes needed in strong winds if you're casting distances. A good average would be size 4 or 5. If you think you need to get further out, hunt for any one of the many silver spinners that has a heavier, bullet–like body. Some of these can easily reach 80m (260ft) or

There are times, in harbours especially, that mullet shoal up and absolutely swarm after food. In this case, bread would be the bait to use but sometimes tiny spinners laced with pieces of ragworm are also attacked.

so. You will be retrieving your spinner quite quickly, so make sure that you have at least one swivel down the line to stop the line kinking. If you don't put the swivel on you'll find line twist becomes unmanageable after 10 to 15 minutes fishing.

Choose a day when the wind has been offshore for quite a while. This will mean that the close–in water is likely to be comparatively clear, allowing the mackerel to see your spinner more easily. If the wind is onshore, it will cloud up and the mackerel won't be able to hunt as effectively and will, therefore, be further out.

Obviously, one of your biggest problems here is actually locating the shoals of fish. Oftentimes, they're hanging a bit further out in slightly deeper water but they will frequently come in close enough for you to get at them. This is especially the case early and late. If you can get out then and if conditions are calm enough, you might well see fish moving on the surface. Look out, also, for the activity of seabirds, and even seals. If you see any surface commotion, get yourself there quickly.

This isn't the most thrilling of fishing – casting and retrieving pretty quickly. But it is super–thrilling when you locate a school of mackerel. You won't believe how hard even a 450–900g (1–2lb) fish fights. These really are the mini–racehorses of the sea and you'll have a spectacular fight on your hands. My own feeling is that there is nothing wrong in taking one or two or even three fish away to feed the family. But I suggest that you resist wholesale slaughter. Of course it's

> 66 *Your ordinary freshwater spinning gear can prove a really exciting way into exploring the sea.* 99

tempting if you're lucky enough to hit a large number of fish and you're catching but remember supplies aren't inexhaustible. Mind you, nothing tastes better than a freshly caught, freshly grilled mackerel. It will make you realize exactly why you are a fisherman.

Sea Bass Fly-fishing for sea bass is hugely exciting but it does demand more skill than fishing for them with lures. You'll find that bass will pick up small spinners that you're casting out for mackerel but they'll also hunt out bigger lures. Silver spoons are good. So are plugs. I have had big success on silvery-coloured shad raps. You can cast these for kilometres and bring them back in a slow, erratic fashion that bass seem to love. Another favourite of mine is the Rapala saltwater skitter pop. This is a super-buoyant, top-water lure equipped with special treble hooks that show resistance to seawater for up to 60 hours. You're best fishing these in very still conditions so that they make a real wake on the surface of the sea.

It's just like fishing for mackerel: you are best waiting until the wind has been offshore so that the water close in is clear. Frequently, bass will chase a surface popper without actually taking it. No matter, at least they are giving away their position, and location is 90 per cent of the game

A lovely sea bass pictured next to the plug that was its downfall. Bass like this one, around about 5 pounds (2.2kg) in weight, are great opportunistic feeders, combing the shoreline for worms, crabs and any small fish that they can come across. This is why plugs and spinners work so well.

You'll find bass wherever there are features, because wherever there are features there is food upon which they thrive. The groynes, sea defences and rocky outcrops harbour endless crabs and tiny fish, while the freshwater stream brings all manner of food items from the village just inland.

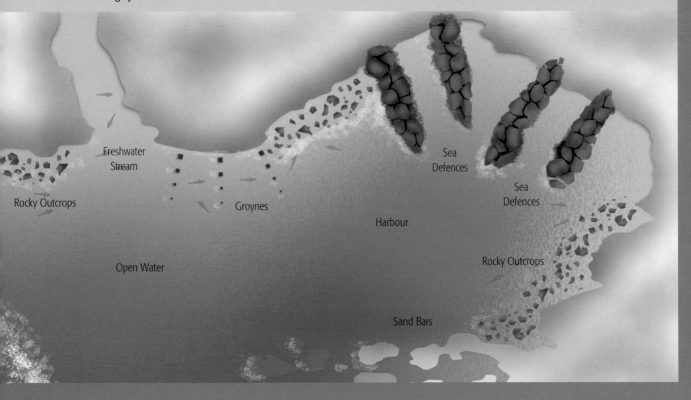

Freshwater Stream

Rocky Outcrops

Groynes

Harbour

Sea Defences

Sea Defences

Rocky Outcrops

Open Water

Sand Bars

here. You can then put on a spinner or an underwater plug and reap your harvest.

Look for sea bass in all the same places that you would if you were fly-fishing for them. Anywhere there are rocks, unusual currents, streams entering, marinas, bridges… anything that says food to a marauding shoal of bass.

When you are bass fishing, it certainly pays to keep on the move. Don't flog a particular area unless you are seeing fish, getting knocks or have a real feeling that there are going to be fish along soon. Don't forget that you won't always get big bangs from bass. Sometimes you will just feel plucks and taps. When this happens, you're better off changing spinner or plug to try and provoke a more solid, aggressive take.

Beach fishing   Whether you're fishing the beach for mackerel or bass – or even pollock come to that – you are well advised to wear a pair of breathable chest waders. Because they are breathable and light, you won't notice that you've got them on and you can walk for kilometres in even the warmest weather. What they do allow

you to do is to get out that crucial 5–10m (15–30ft) to achieve just a bit more casting distance. They are also great for when a fish comes to hand and you need to unhook it and return it without taking it onto the shingle. Remember, even though the sea is a big place, fish stocks aren't always enormous and conservation should always be well up in your mind.

Sea Trout   These fish are eminently catchable on small plugs and spinners, especially in creeks and estuaries where freshwater is running in. Often sea trout will run these streams to spawn. They'll certainly investigate them looking for food stocks, such as sticklebacks and the fry of all the cyprinid species. This makes them very vulnerable indeed to an attack with a spinner. Once again, something small and silver frequently does the trick.

The best time for this is, once more, early or late in the day – I have a particular liking for dusk and the first hour or so of darkness. But, of course, the tide is also important. Often, sea trout will enter these estuaries in huge numbers when the tide is

Scan the surface for movement. If you do see anything, cast quickly because all fish in the sea tend to feed and move in fast, fluid movements and simply don't hang about. If you delay, you risk missing the shoal. Cast along the beach rather than aimlessly out into the sea… remember that fish are frequently found in the surf itself.

Sea trout come into rivers to feed and especially to breed. They tend to lie doggo during the day but as the sun sinks and the night sets in, they move upriver, often foraging as they go.

on the flood (rising). Sometimes, they will follow water that is only a few centimetres deep. They will explore ditches and dykes while the water is high and drop back into the main estuary as the tide begins to ebb. So, in essence, you can hit them as they're coming in with the tide and then when they are going out as it drops.

Once again, it pays to keep on the move and, especially, look out for signs of feeding fish. You'll often see them bow waving on the surface as they chase small fry around. Look, too, for the signs of skittering fish making their escape.

Remember that some of these sea trout can be very large indeed. The vast majority will probably be between half and 1.5kg (1–3lb) in weight but 4.5kg (10lb) or larger fish aren't that uncommon. For this reason, I wouldn't suggest dropping much beneath 10–12lb breaking strain when it comes to line choice.

Lures Remember that most sea species will take a lure at some time or another. Pollock, for example, are susceptible around rocky headlands. If you can get close enough to a cod, then a silver lure will be engulfed. And if you're lucky enough to head to more exotic climes you will find tarpon, especially, hit lures dramatically. However, this is all just a bit in the future for the beginner. Make your first steps sure, confident ones, and save the Silver King until you've got a good few species of decent size under your belt.

Sea fishing in the northern hemisphere often gets better the more remote you become. Certainly, the north of Scotland can provide tremendous sport around islands and rocky outcrops.

Moving Onwards and Upwards

Obviously, the more fishing experiences that you enjoy, the more your knowledge will build up. But, importantly, it helps if you're catching things. Blank sessions can help you to some degree, but if all you are experiencing is blanks, it becomes hard to learn any real lessons. When you're learning, you're better fishing easier waters for easier fish. Frequent successes help you to build up a picture of your progress and to understand why you might sometimes do better and sometimes worse. There's plenty of time for the hard waters when you're more experienced and have more faith in your ability.

Keeping a diary Make sure that all your progress counts. I still keep a fishing diary. It's amazing how often you forget details of a day without some very positive reminder. Often, a small detail can mean the difference between success and failure. If you note down everything that happens to you through a session, you will stand much more chance of remembering the fine detail and building up a picture of your developing angling career.

Photographs Taking photographs can make your diary more fun and more personal. The advent of digital cameras means that photography has never been easier or cheaper. It's often rewarding to photograph fish close up, in great detail. You might find that you catch these fish again in years to come and you will then have an idea of how they have grown or are developing. All pike, for example, have different spotting patterns, as individual as our fingerprints. Carp have individual scale patterns. Most other species will also have one or two identifying features, enabling you to recognize them again at a later date. This might be a malformed fin perhaps, or an irregular scale pattern. Remember that we're more than mere fish catchers, we're also fish detectives.

More information There's a whole world of information out there to carry you along after you've finished this book. Virtually all of today's magazines are packed with great ideas, presented in a very accessible form. The Internet is full of information. Books are dearest companions. There are lots of DVDs out now which give hard, hands-on advice. It's a great idea to go out with a guide

or even on a fishing course. Never neglect your tackle dealer. A walk along a bank and a chat with older, or more experienced anglers is bound to help. You can join a club – this will give you access to private or protected waters. You might find that the club has open evenings with a visiting lecturer. In years to come, you might become part of a syndicate on a water that's even more exclusive. It could well be that you and your syndicate members form a brotherhood and that the depth of your knowledge will increase hugely and quickly.

Fishing holidays Don't ignore the possibility of a fishing holiday. For some reason, seven days spent fishing each day consecutively does you a lot more good than seven days split up over a couple of months. Somehow you get into a rhythm. You enter a zone. You begin to become more confident. You're happier with your tackle. You begin to see some continuity in the fishing sessions as they develop. The constant living and breathing of the sport does nothing but help you learn at an increased pace.

Go deeper Learning shouldn't just be about information and results. Become involved with some of the conservation bodies, perhaps. Or take part in river restoration projects. These are hugely rewarding and you are paying back something to the environment you glory in. Not all angling literature is how-to books; there is also deep, significant literature that is more impressive than in any other sport – bar none. One of my favourites is *Going Fishing* by Negley Farson. The book has been around for well over half a century but is still magnificent. More recently, *Casting at the Sun* by Christopher Yates is a brilliant piece of work and, I'm humble to say, my own *Trout at Ten Thousand Feet* has reaped some praise. There's a spiritual side to angling which I'm sure you will develop as the seasons progress.

66 *Now just go and enjoy yourself.* 99

Glossary

Avons Common river floats that are good for use in fast moving water at longish distances.

Backstop A small shot placed up the line and above the float to make the line less vulnerable to surface drift.

Barbless hooks A hook made without a barb and therefore easier to unhook and less harmful to the fish.

Block end feeder A plastic tube feeder with its ends covered and holes around the side in order to slow down the rate at which bait is released.

Boilies Carefully prepared small balls of man–made bait that are available in a range of colours and flavours.

Braid line A fishing line made from very strong braided man–made fibres and largely resistant to abrasion.

Breaking strain The point at which the fishing line breaks.

Casting The act of throwing a fishing line out over the water. The usual technique is to flick the line behind you and then out towards the water.

Casters Refers to the chrysalis stage between maggots and bluebottles.

Centre Pin Reel A traditional type of reel for use on rivers. It features a large rotating spool. The flow of the water provides enough inertia to take the line off this rotating spool.

Chest waders Waterproof boots that extend from the foot to the chest and allow you to stand further out in the water.

Coarse Fish All freshwater fish except Salmon and Trout are coarse fish.

Coarse Fishing Coarse fishing is advanced freshwater fishing. It includes the many different techniques and methods that are used to catch coarse fish. Techniques classified as coarse fishing include float fishing, pole fishing, bait fishing, lure fishing etc.

Crease An area in the water where slow and fast moving water meets.

Cyprinids These are the largest family of fresh–water fish and are made up of 2,420 species including carp and barbel.

Disgourger A tool to help remove hooks from a fish's mouth.

Double taper A common type of fly line. The line tapers at either end and is at its thickest in the middle.

Feathering An act in fishing whereby you place your finger on the reel spool to slow down the speed at which the line comes off it.

Fishing vest A very useful item of clothing with many pockets for storing fishing equipment. Particularly practical for fly fishing.

Fixed spool reel One of the most popular types of spool, characterised by a bale arm, a handle for retrieving the line, a rear drag and an anti–reverse lever.

Floatant A liquid used to coat a fishing line in order to help it float on the surface of the water.

Groundbait Food that is thrown into the water to attract and keep fish around your hook bait. The type of groundbait used depends on the fish targetted and conditions. Bread crumb is the most common form of groundbait.

Hair rig The act of tying a bait to the hook using a hair, rather than putting the bait directly onto the hook itself.

Halibut pellet A type of bait that is attached to the hook by means of elastic bands or hair rigs. Excellent for many river species and for carp.

Landing net A net used to carry a hooked fish from the water to the bank. Net heads come in many shapes and sizes depending on the fish targetted.

Legering A method of fishing using a weight to keep bait on the river bed for fish that are expected to feed there.

Lure An object attached to the end of a fishing line and designed to look like fish's prey. A lure is equipped with a hook that will catch the fish when it attacks.

Marker Float A float that is cast out into the area of water you have baited up to indicate where best to put your bait hook.

Monofilament A type of line made up of one single strand of nylon.

Multiplier reel Also commonly known as a bait casting reel, these function using the weight of a bait or lure as it pulls on the line and turns the spool to release more line. The heavier the lure, the longer the cast.

Polaroid glasses An essential piece of equipment that helps to minimize the surface glare from the sun's reflection on the water and into your eyes.

Pre-Baiting The act of throwing in free bait offerings into the area of water you want to fish later in the day (or next day), in order to mislead the fish into thinking it is a good area to feed.

Priest A type of mallet used for despatching fish. As the weight of the mallet is well balanced and specially designed, they are more humane than a rock from the river bank.

Quiver tip A very sensitive rod tip useful in detecting bites.

Rod rest A device allowing you to rest your rod rather than holding it. Essential for lengthy sessions.

Seat box A specially designed box that doubles as a handy storage box and comfortable seat.

Shot Small metal balls traditionally made from lead but now more commonly made of non-toxic alternatives, which are cut halfway through to enable them to be attached to the line to add weight.

Spod A large plastic container packed full of bait that is tied to the heavy line of a stout rod.

Stick float Type of float attached to the line at the top, middle and bottom of the float by silicone rubbers, allowing the float to move with the main flow of the water.

Strike indicator A piece of polystyrene attached to the line that indicate a bite.

Swim The place where you are fishing.

Trotting A method of fishing in rivers using a stick float that allows the float to behave naturally among the flow of the downstream.

Test curve rating The amount of weight required to put a rod under pressure and bend to its greatest extent.

Wagglers Types of freshwater float attached through an eye. There are three types of waggler floats; Insert wagglers, used in slow-flowing water such as canals, bodied wagglers that are used for casting long distances on lakes, and crystal wagglers that are invisible to fish.

Index